Free As Air

A Musical in Two Acts

Dorothy Reynolds and Julian Slade

A Samuel French Acting Edition

SAMUELFRENCH-LONDON.CO.UK
SAMUELFRENCH.COM

Music and Lyrics Copyright © 1959 by Francis, Day, and Hunter, Ltd
Copyright © Acting Edition 1960 by Samuel French Ltd
All Rights Reserved

FREE AS AIR is fully protected under the copyright laws of the British Commonwealth, including Canada, the United States of America, and all other countries of the Copyright Union. All rights, including professional and amateur stage productions, recitation, lecturing, public reading, motion picture, radio broadcasting, television and the rights of translation into foreign languages are strictly reserved.

ISBN 978-0-573-08014-2

www.samuelfrench-london.co.uk

www.samuelfrench.com

FOR AMATEUR PRODUCTION ENQUIRIES

UNITED KINGDOM AND WORLD EXCLUDING NORTH AMERICA

plays@SamuelFrench-London.co.uk

020 7255 4302/01

Each title is subject to availability from Samuel French, depending upon country of performance.

CAUTION: Professional and amateur producers are hereby warned that *FREE AS AIR* is subject to a licensing fee. Publication of this play does not imply availability for performance. Both amateurs and professionals considering a production are strongly advised to apply to the appropriate agent before starting rehearsals, advertising, or booking a theatre. A licensing fee must be paid whether the title is presented for charity or gain and whether or not admission is charged.

The professional rights in this play are controlled by The Agency Ltd, 24 Pottery Lane, Holland Park, London W11 4LZ.

No one shall make any changes in this title for the purpose of production. No part of this book may be reproduced, stored in a retrieval system, or transmitted in any form, by any means, now known or yet to be invented, including mechanical, electronic, photocopying, recording, videotaping, or otherwise, without the prior written permission of the publisher. No one shall upload this title, or part of this title, to any social media websites.

The right of Dorothy Reynolds and Julian Slade to be identified as author of this work has been asserted by them in accordance with Section 77 of the Copyright, Designs and Patents Act 1988

FREE AS AIR

Presented by Linnet and Dunfee Ltd at The Savoy Theatre, London, on the 6th June, 1957, with the following cast of characters—
(in the order of their appearance)

MOLLY	*Patricia Bredin*
MR MUTCH, the shopkeeper	*Roy Godfrey*
MR POTTER, the bailiff	*Howard Goorney*
MISS CATAMOLE	*Dorothy Reynolds*
GREGORY, Bindweed's assistant	*Donald Bradley*
CONNIE ⎫	*Joyce Carpenter*
MARY ⎪	*Mary Benning*
FLO ⎬ Island Girls	*Patricia Somerset*
SUSIE ⎪	*Evelyne Anderson*
JEAN ⎪	*Jean Marion Taylor*
ABBIE ⎭	*Dawn Fryer*
MARK ⎫	*Malcolm Farquhar*
JOHN ⎬ Island Men	*Len Rossiter*
MATT ⎭	*Raymond Parks*
BINDWEED, the gardener	*Vincent Charles*
LORD PAUL POSTUMOUS, the Lord of the Manor	*Michael Aldridge*
TOM FERRIER, a boatman	*Bill Tasker*
GERALDINE MELFORD, an heiress	*Gillian Lewis*
ALBERT POSTUMOUS, Lord Paul's nephew	*John Trevor*
FRANÇOIS, the barman	*Donald Bradley*
IVY CRUSH, a woman reporter	*Josephine Tewson*
JACK AMERSHAM, a racing motorist	*Gerald Harper*
1ST REPORTER	*Malcolm Farquhar*
2ND REPORTER	*Len Rossiter*
3RD REPORTER	*Raymond Parks*

CHORUS OF ISLANDERS, MECHANICS AND SUPPORTERS

Directed by DENIS CAREY
Musical Numbers staged by MARK STUART
Décor by PATRICK ROBERTSON
Orchestration by PETER KNIGHT

SYNOPSIS OF SCENES

The action passes on the islands of Terhou and Jersey in May of the present year

ACT I

SCENE 1 The Well on Terhou. Morning
SCENE 2 Front Cloth
SCENE 3 The Seashore. Morning
SCENE 4 Island Front Cloth. Later the same morning
SCENE 5 Exterior of Shop and Miss Catamole's House. The afternoon of the same day
SCENE 6 Island Front Cloth. Early the same evening
SCENE 7 The Bar of the Octopus Hotel, Jersey. Later the same evening
SCENE 8 Island Front Cloth. Later the same night
SCENE 9 Exterior of Shop and Miss Catamole's House. Immediately following

ACT II

SCENE 1 The terrace of the Big House. The following morning
SCENE 2 Front Cloth
SCENE 3 The Well. Later the same morning
SCENE 4 Island Front Cloth. The afternoon of the same day
SCENE 5 The Seashore. Later that afternoon
SCENE 6 Island Front Cloth. Later that afternoon
SCENE 7 The Bar of the Octopus Hotel. Early evening of the same day
SCENE 8 Island Front Cloth. A little later that evening
SCENE 9 The Well. Sunset

MUSIC

ACT I

		Overture and opening music	
No.	1	" I'm Up Early "	Molly and Islanders
No.	2	Reprise. " I'm Up Early "	Potter, Mutch, Lord Paul and Chorus
No.	3	" Let the Grass Grow "	Mutch, Potter and Lord Paul
No.	3a	Dance and Reprise. " Let the Grass Grow "	Mutch, Potter and Lord Paul
No.	4	" Nothing But Sea and Sky "	Geraldine and Chorus
No.	5	" The Boat's In "	Islanders
No.	6	" Free to Sing "	Albert and Geraldine
No.	6a	Exit music	
No.	7	" A Man From The Mainland "	Molly
No.	8	Reprise. " Free to Sing "	Ensemble
No.	9	Exit music	
No.	10	Hurry music	
No.	11	Reprise. " Nothing but Sea and Sky "	Geraldine and Albert
No.	11a	" Daily Echo "	Ivy and Ensemble
No.	12	" Her Mummy Doesn't Like Me Any More "	Jack and Chorus
No.	13	Reprise. " The Boat's In "	Lord Paul, Ivy and Jack
No.	14	" The Girl from London "	Ensemble

ACT II

No.	15	Opening music	
No.	16	Reprise. " A Man From The Mainland "	Molly, Jack and Girls
No.	17	" I'd Like To Be Like You "	Albert and Geraldine
No.	18	" Testudo "	Ensemble
No.	19	" I've Got My Feet On The Ground "	Jack and Molly
No.	20	" Holiday Island " (Part I)	Ensemble
No.	20a	" Holiday Island " (Part II)	Ensemble
No.	20b	Reprise. " Holiday Island " Change of Scene	

FREE AS AIR

No. 21	Geraldine's exit	
No. 21a	Hurry music	
No. 22	"Geraldine"	Reporters
No. 23	Reprise. "Free To Sing"	Ensemble
No. 24	"We're Holding Hands"	Miss Catamole and Potter
No. 25	"Terhou"	Molly and The Company
No. 26	Finale	The Company

CURTAIN CALLS

No. 27	Reprise. "I'm Up Early"	The Company
No. 28	Reprise. "A Man From The Mainland"	The Company
No. 29	Reprise. "Let The Grass Grow"	The Company

PLAY-OUT MUSIC

| No. 30 | Reprise. "I'm Up Early" | |

FREE AS AIR

ACT I

Scene 1

The Well on Terhou. A morning in May.

Across the back is a low, broken wall with the sea beyond. In front of the wall, from R to L there is a rocky path with rough steps at each end. Miss Catamole's house is R and Mr Potter's house is L. The well is C. There is a bench R and a stool L. On the bench there is a milk-jug with a beaded cover and three tea-towels spread out to dry. On the stool there is a small metal milk-churn. A fishing-net is hanging on a bridle up R and there are three fish-boxes and a basket of seaweed on the wall up L. There is a bucket at the well.

OVERTURE AND OPENING MUSIC

When the CURTAIN *rises, it is just after sunrise.* MOLLY *is seated on the wall up* R. MR MUTCH *enters up* L, *carrying a small milk-churn and ladle. He goes to the churn on the stool and ladles milk into it.*

MOLLY [*speaking over the music*] Good morning, Mr Mutch.
MUTCH. Good morning, Molly, you're up early.
MOLLY. Yes, it's the great day tomorrow.
MUTCH. We hope so. [*He crosses and ladles milk into the jug on the stool* R]

MR POTTER *enters from his house* L, *wearing shirt, shoes, hat and pyjama trousers. He picks up the small churn from the stool.*

MOLLY. Good morning, Mr Potter, it's the great day tomorrow.
POTTER. Is it?

POTTER *exits into his house* L.

MISS CATAMOLE *enters up* L *and crosses to Mutch.*

"I'M UP EARLY"   No. 1

MOLLY AND ISLANDERS

MUTCH [*speaking over the music*] 'Morning, Miss Catamole.
MISS CATAMOLE. It's the great day tomorrow.
MUTCH. So they say.

MUTCH *hands Miss Catamole the jug from the bench and exits up* R.

MISS CATAMOLE. Molly, I've never seen you up so early.
MOLLY [*rising*] I never have been. [*She comes down the steps* R *to the well*]

MISS CATAMOLE *puts the jug on the bench and folds the tea-towels.*

MOLLY [*singing*] Isn't it surprising,
The sun is barely rising,
And I'm awake already.
This energy is crazy,
I feel a little hazy,
I'm reckless, I'm unsteady,
But how could I stay in bed?
Tomorrow lies ahead.

1

It's a great day
And it's on its way
That's why I'm wide awake today.

[*She crosses to the bench and dips her finger in the milk-jug*]

        Miss Catamole *snatches up the jug and exits* R.

        Potter *enters from his house with a small bowl and a towel and goes to the well to wash.*

I'm up early
To greet the day
To smell the air, to feel the breeze,
To hear the rustling in the trees
This morning.
I'm up early,
I couldn't sleep.

[*She wanders to the well and sits on the step, facing front*]

        Gregory *enters up* L *and crosses on the rostrum to* C. *He carries a spade and a duster. He sees Molly, and joins her on the step.*

I woke up dreaming something sweet;
I'll smile at ev'ryone I meet
This morning.
Ev'rywhere
A stir is in the air.
Ev'rything
Is telling me it's Spring.

        Three Island Men *and six* Island Girls *enter in twos and threes, carrying fish-baskets, brooms, bowls, scrubbing brushes and washing-baskets with washing.*

I'm up early
To see the sun.
I know that he is here to stay,
I know it's what I mean by May
This morning,
Because it's that kind of a morning
This morning.

        Miss Catamole *enters* R. *She carries her knitting-bag and two cups of tea.* Potter *crosses to her and they sit on the bench* R. Miss Catamole *gives a cup of tea to Potter, puts the other on the bench beside her and begins to knit.*

Men.   We're up early,
We don't know why,
But someone said we should be up
When tea is made we need a cup
This morning.

Girls.   We're up early
To make our plans,
We know we've got a lot to do;
We're not so sure of what to do
This morning.

        Bindweed *enters up* R *and moves* RC.

SCENE 1	FREE AS AIR	

ALL. What a change!
      Today is very strange.
      By mistake
      The island's wide awake.

BINDWEED. I'm up early,

> MOLLY *rises and faces* BINDWEED. GREGORY *rises, moves to the well up* R *and sits.*

And I woke up
With swarms of bees inside my head.
I wish I could have stayed in bed
This morning.
Because it's that kind of a morning
This morning.

ALL. Every morning for that old bore
      Is the morning after the night before.

> MOLLY *moves to watch* GIRLS *packing fish. She eyes the* ISLAND MEN. *Two of them move to* MOLLY *and carry her to their fish-baskets.*

We're up early
To mend our shoes—
To brush our hair and paint our door—
To clean our windows, wash our floor
This morning.
We're up early
To feed the hens
To scrub the pigs and milk the cow
To pot a lobster, speed the plough
This morning.

> *An* ISLAND MAN *brings some fish-boxes down* L. *One* GIRL *moves down to them and picks a fish from her basket. Three* GIRLS *take clothes from a basket down* R *and wash them. One* GIRL *runs gaily round showing off a new petticoat which she holds to her waist.*

Everyone
Has something to be done
Work today
Tomorrow we will play.

We're up early
To toil and spin
To work until tomorrow comes
We won't be twiddling any thumbs
This morning.
It isn't that kind of a morning
Not that kind of a morning
Not that kind of a morning
This morning

> MUTCH *enters up* R *and comes down* C.

1ST GIRL. Good morning, Mr Mutch. It's the great day tomorrow.
MUTCH. I do wish everyone would stop saying that. There may not be an Independence Day tomorrow at all, for goodness' sake. Is everyone here?
MISS CATAMOLE. Except Lord Paul and Mr Albert.

MUTCH. Ah well, no doubt they'll be down as soon as they're up. Now! What is the most important feature of our celebrations? [MUSIC]
2ND GIRL. The food.
3RD GIRL. The crowning of an island Queen, Mr Mutch.
POTTER. The crowning of an island what?
MISS CATAMOLE. Queen.
MUTCH. Precisely. Now, the law clearly states that no young woman may be crowned more than once, and all you young ladies, you've already been Queen, haven't you?
1ST GIRL. Nineteen forty-eight.
2ND GIRL. Nineteen fifty-one.
3RD GIRL. Nineteen fifty.
MOLLY. 'Fifty-four.
4TH GIRL. 'Fifty-six.
MISS CATAMOLE [*cheerfully*] 'Twenty-seven.
MUTCH. There you are, you see? Coronation tomorrow and no Queen. It's a crisis.

MOLLY sits on the wall up C.

POTTER. Oh, good! Then we shall have to have an extraordinary meeting of Parliament.
MUTCH. We can't meet without Lord Paul.
MISS CATAMOLE [*to one of the Girls*] Go and see if he's awake.
GREGORY [*looking off* R] Here he is. Here's Lord Paul.

LORD PAUL POSTUMOUS *enters up* R *on the rostrum and crosses to* LC. *He carries a walking-stick, a telescope and a megaphone.*

LORD PAUL. 'Morning, Mutch. 'Morning, all. 'Morning, Potter. [*He looks through the telescope*] Boat in yet?
MISS CATAMOLE. Not yet.
LORD PAUL. Has she been sighted?
POTTER. I don't think so.
LORD PAUL. Well, keep a good look out. [*He moves to exit* L]
MUTCH [*stopping Lord Paul*] Lord Paul, please. There's a crisis. The island's run out of young women.
LORD PAUL. Surely you exaggerate.

LORD PAUL *and* MUTCH *move down* LC.

MUTCH. We have no-one to enact the Queen tomorrow.
POTTER. So we think you should call Parliament.
LORD PAUL. Very well. [*He calls through the megaphone*] Parliament!
POTTER [*rising and moving down* LC] We're all here.

REPRISE

No. 2

"I'M UP EARLY"

POTTER, MUTCH, LORD PAUL and CHORUS

LORD PAUL, POTTER and MUTCH
    We're up early
    To find a Queen
    To search the hills
    To scour the plains
    To rack our overheated brains
    This morning.

SCENE 1   FREE AS AIR

ALL.	We're up early	MUSIC
	To join the search	
	We thought the day began so well	
	But then again you just can't tell	
	This morning.	
	We're up early to join the search	
	One girl missing, we're in the lurch.	
	We can see today will be	
	A busy day for	
LORD PAUL.	Me	
POTTER.	And me	
MUTCH.	And me	
1ST GIRL	And me	
2ND GIRL.	And me	
MAN	And me	
MOLLY.	And me	
ALL.	Because it's that kind of a morning	
	It's that kind of a morning	
	It's that kind of a morning	
	This morning.	

                  MISS CATAMOLE *and* GREGORY *rise and exit* R.

                  MOLLY, BINDWEED *and three* MEN *exit up* R.

                  Three GIRLS *exit up* L, *and three* GIRLS *exit down* R. *All take their baskets, etc., with them.* POTTER *moves up* L, *picks up the basket of seaweed from the wall, brings it to the stool* L *and sits.* MUTCH *moves the bench* R *nearer the well, sits and lights his pipe.* LORD PAUL *moves to the well.* POTTER *sorts the seaweed.*

MUTCH. Potter, must you be sorting seaweed?
POTTER. It's got to be done. Besides, it helps me to concentrate.
LORD PAUL. Is Parliament sitting? [*He sits* L *of Mutch on the bench*]
MUTCH. I declare this meeting open. [*He invites Lord Paul to speak*] Lord Paul . . . ?
LORD PAUL. I've thought it all out. As we have no young woman to enact the Queen tomorrow, it becomes my duty to go to the mainland and find one.
MUTCH. No! Whenever there's a crisis you always go running away.
LORD PAUL. Running away?
MUTCH. No-one ever leaves the island except you.
LORD PAUL. Well, they should. Our attitude to the mainland should be one of humility   All I go for is to seek improvements.
MUTCH. And all you bring back is a hangover and a hunted look.

                  LORD PAUL *rises and moves on to the rostrum up* C.

POTTER. I've got a solution.
MUTCH. You have?
POTTER. Yes. You can't make a new woman, so you make a new law.
MUTCH. Obvious.
POTTER. Simply saying . . .
LORD PAUL. Someone's got to go to the mainland.
MUTCH. I don't see why. Bailiff.
POTTER. Simply saying that a young woman can be Queen twice.
MUTCH. There, Lord Paul. I told you it wasn't necessary to go to the mainland. Now, let's get the new law written down. Then we can knock off for the day.
POTTER. I've just remembered. We've run out of ink. Would pencil . . . ?
MUTCH. Certainly not. Lord Paul?
LORD PAUL. No. The island's right out of ink.
POTTER. So until the boat comes in . . .
MUTCH. There's nothing we can do. We'd better go down and meet it.

LORD PAUL. She's not in sight, yet.
POTTER [*rising*] Good. Then we can go slowly.
MUTCH [*rising and returning the bench to the wall* R] And take the long way round.

POTTER *picks up the basket and stool and exits with them* L.

"LET THE GRASS GROW" No. 3

MUTCH, POTTER and LORD PAUL

MUTCH *wanders down* L *as he sings*   LORD PAUL *comes down to him*.

MUTCH [*singing*] A man can be so busy, it fairly makes you dizzy,
As if he were a badger or a bee.
All the big sensational ills are occupational

POTTER *enters* L.

POTTER   Like housemaid's knee.
MUTCH.   He's filling every minute, as if his life was in it,
Hour after hour whizzes past.
But life is very nice and I'd like to give advice
On how to spin it out and make it last.

ALL.   Let the grass grow under your feet
Till it grows knee deep.
Let the bright day amble along
Till it ends in sleep.
A man's life is very quickly over,
Make time last by wandering through the clover.
Let the grass grow under your feet,
Give it a chance to grow until it grows knee deep.

LORD PAUL.   Deeper, deeper, deeper, deeper, deeper, deeper, deeper.
ALL.   Give it a chance to grow until it grows knee deep.
LORD PAUL.   Give it a chance to grow
ALL.   Knee deep.

They wander R, *turn up stage and amble across to* L.

Let the grass grow under your feet
Till it grows waist high.
Let the breezes blow as they will,
Let the day drift by.
A man's life is longer if he lazes.
Make time last by wandering through the daisies.
Let the grass grow under your feet
Give it a chance to grow until it grows waist high.

LORD PAUL.   Higher, higher, higher, higher, higher, higher, higher.
ALL.   Give it a chance to grow until it grows waist high
LORD PAUL.   Give it a chance to grow
ALL.   Waist high.

The FRONT CLOTH *falls*

SCENE 2

A Gorse Front Cloth

DANCE and REPRISE

"LET THE GRASS GROW"

No. 3a

MUTCH, POTTER and LORD PAUL

MUTCH, POTTER and LORD PAUL *re-enter in front of the Front Cloth for a dance routine and reprise of the number.*

ALL. Let the grass grow under your feet
Till it grows knee deep.
Let the bright day amble along
Till it ends in sleep.
A man's life is very quickly over,
Make time last by wandering through the clover.
Let the grass grow under your feet,
Give it a chance to grow until it grows knee deep.
LORD PAUL. Deeper, deeper, deeper, deeper, deeper, deeper, deeper.
ALL. Give it a chance to grow until it grows knee deep.
LORD PAUL. Give it a chance to grow
ALL. Knee deep.

MUTCH, POTTER *and* LORD PAUL *exit.*

SCENE 3

The Seashore. Morning.

Across the back is a low, broken wall with the sea beyond. In front of the wall, from R *to* L *there is a rocky path with rough steps* R. *There is a small upturned boat* LC *and the mast of another boat can be seen behind the wall up* C. *Fishing-nets are draped on the wall to dry and there are two lobster pots* R.

When the FRONT CLOTH *rises,* TOM FERRIER *is on the rostrum up* R, *with his back to the audience, leaning over the wall. Two suitcases are on the ground beside him. A smaller case is handed up to him, and he puts it with the others.*

TOM. You can come up, there's no-one about.

GERALDINE MELFORD, *assisted by* TOM, *climbs over the wall.*

GERALDINE. What do you mean? Aren't visitors allowed?
TOM [*shrugging*] They never come.
GERALDINE. No. I didn't even know there was an island here. I must pay you for the trip. [*She opens her handbag*]
TOM [*waving it away; unsmiling*] I'd got to come, anyway. [*He turns* R *to go*]
GERALDINE. How often does your boat go to the mainland?
TOM [*stopping and turning*] Once a month.
GERALDINE. Then I'm all right for a bit. Do you think there's anywhere I can stay?

"NOTHING BUT SEA AND SKY"

GERALDINE AND CHORUS

No. 4

TOM [*over the music*] I don't know. You'd better stop here.

TOM *exits* R. GERALDINE *moves* L, *removes her coat, puts it on the upturned boat, then moves* C.

GERALDINE [*singing*] This is what I meant, MUSIC
The nights I dreamed,
Of a peaceful land
Where nothing seemed
To be worrying me,
Or hurrying me.
Yes, this is why
I have longed so long for the sea and the sky

Nothing but sea and sky,
And a seagull flying by,
And a lonely beach with nobody here but me—
This is where I seem
A part of my dream,
Suddenly I'm alone and free!
Nothing but sea and sand
And a seashell in my hand,
And a hazy blue as far as the eye can see.
I could stay all day
And gaze at the spray,
Knowing that I'm alone and free.

Shimmering sky
Over a gentle sea!
I'm on my own
And glad to be
Where there is
Nothing but sea and sky,
And the world so still that I
Only hear the water whispering peace to me.

CHORUS [*off*] Ah—Ah—Ah—Ah—Ah!

GERALDINE. I can hear the waves
And echoing caves
Telling me I'm alone and free.

MISS CATAMOLE *enters up* R *and comes* RC. *She carries her knitting.*

MISS CATAMOLE [*seeing Geraldine*] Oh! Ha, ha, ha, ha, ha, ha! I beg pardon. You gave me such a shock.
GERALDINE. I'm sorry.
MISS CATAMOLE. No, it made a nice change. Well, I never did! I'm Miss Catamole. Who are you?
GERALDINE. I'm Miss Melford.
MISS CATAMOLE. Are you staying long?
GERALDINE. Tom wasn't sure whether I'd be allowed to stay at all.

MISS CATAMOLE *sits on a lobster-pot and knits.*

MISS CATAMOLE. No. I think there is a law somewhere. I seem to remember when I was a girl someone was even forbidden to land.
GERALDINE. Oh. You mean I shouldn't have come here?
MISS CATAMOLE. Oh, no, it's lovely. I expect there's a way of making you legitimate.

GERALDINE *crosses and sits on the boat.*

SCENE 8   FREE AS AIR

MUTCH, POTTER and LORD PAUL enter up R, singing and dancing, TOM dancing in their wake. LORD PAUL is piping on a recorder. MUTCH is leading. They cross L on the rostrum, step down, cross R, mount the steps, turn and start to come down. MUTCH sees Geraldine and stops suddenly. POTTER, LORD PAUL and TOM pile up behind him. MUTCH hides behind the wing up R.

POTTER [*moving towards Geraldine*] Good morning. I've come for the ink.

                     POTTER exits up L.

LORD PAUL [*doffing his hat*] Good morning. Welcome! Welcome! I'm Lord Paul Postumous. You're from the mainland. I can see that, of course. I sometimes go to the mainland myself.
GERALDINE. Really?
LORD PAUL [*moving to Geraldine*] To seek improvements, you know. But if I may say so, you're the best improvement that ever landed here.
GERALDINE. Thank you.
LORD PAUL [*crossing to L of Geraldine*] Wish I'd landed you myself.
MISS CATAMOLE. Mr Mutch, it's quite safe to come out.

                     MUTCH emerges.

MUTCH [*moving to R of Geraldine*] Safe? *I* know it's safe. But there's a law against this lady.
MISS CATAMOLE. This is Miss Melford.
GERALDINE. How do you do?
MUTCH. Oh, I usually do pretty well. But there's a law . . .

           TOM suddenly utters a piercing whistle and beckons off R.

[*He rounds on Tom*] Ssssh!

          LORD PAUL takes GERALDINE by the arm and leads her down L

LORD PAUL. I live up there at the Big House. It looks white, now, but it's pink in the evenings. I live there with my nephew.
MISS CATAMOLE. Where *is* Mr Albert?
LORD PAUL. Busy. [*He shrugs*] Reading, I expect. [*To Geraldine*] My nephew does a lot of reading.

                 MOLLY runs on up R to C.

MOLLY. What's the matter with Tom? [*She sees Geraldine and stops*] Oh! That dress!
GERALDINE. You like it?
MOLLY [*crossing and circling Geraldine*] And those shoes. [*She sits on the boat*]
MISS CATAMOLE [*looking off L*] Here's Mr Albert.

         ALBERT POSTUMOUS enters L. He is reading a list of names.

I was just saying, Mr Albert, here you are.
ALBERT [*crossing to C*] Yes. G-good morning.
LORD PAUL. Miss Melford. This is my nephew.
GERALDINE [*to Albert*] How are you?
ALBERT. I'm very well, thank you.
LORD PAUL [*to Geraldine*] You'll be our guest, of course.
MISS CATAMOLE [*rising and crossing to Geraldine*] No, Lord Paul. I've got an empty room.

                  TOM moves down R.

MUTCH. Guest? Guest? The word is not *mentioned* in the law. We'll get this straight. [*He searches his pockets busily for pencil and paper*] Now, Miss Melford, who invited you?
TOM [*unexpectedly*] I did.
GERALDINE. Oh, it's not true. I invited myself. I *begged* you . . .
TOM [*stubbornly*] I invited you into my boat.
MISS CATAMOLE. Tom's never brought a passenger before. Why did you, Tom?

                 LORD PAUL crosses to LC.

10 FREE AS AIR ACT I

TOM. I thought she could be the Queen.   MUSIC
GERALDINE. Queen ?
LORD PAUL⎫   ⎧Oh, splendid !
MOLLY   ⎬[together]⎨What a good idea !
MUTCH   ⎭   ⎩It might be managed.
ALBERT. If Miss M-Melford would undertake it.
GERALDINE. But I've no experience of . . .
MISS CATAMOLE. It's our Independence Day tomorrow. We have a Coronation ceremony and no-one to take the part of the Queen.
MOLLY. Because we've all done it before.
GERALDINE. Well, I . . .
MOLLY [rising] Oh, please.
GERALDINE. I should be very honoured. Thank you.
LORD PAUL⎫   ⎧Thank you, Miss Melford.
ALBERT   ⎬[together]⎨It's very k-kind.
MISS CATAMOLE. You've solved our only problem.

POTTER *enters up* C *and crosses to* TOM.

POTTER. Tom, did you bring my bottle of ink ?

"THE BOAT'S IN"   No. 5

ISLANDERS

MISS CATAMOLE [*over the music*] We're just going to unload, Mr Potter. Perhaps Mr Albert would like to show Miss Melford over the island.
ALBERT. C-certainly.
GERALDINE. Thank you.

> *During the introductory lines,* MISS CATAMOLE *exits up* L, *disposes of her knitting and re-enters.* ALBERT *takes* GERALDINE *to the boat, where she sits.* ALBERT *and* LORD PAUL *stand* C. TOM *takes the lobster-pots off* R *and re-enters.* MOLLY *moves up* C. MUTCH *moves up* L *on to the rostrum. An* ISLAND MAN *appears over the wall up* L *and stands on the rostrum.*

ISLAND MAN.   Ay, ay, up there !
FISHERMEN [*off*] Ay, ay, down there !
ISLAND MAN.   The boat's in !
FISHERMEN [*off*] The boat's in !
ISLAND MAN.   We're unloading.
FISHERMEN [*off*] We're unloading.

> *The* CHORUS *enter up* R, *up* L *and down* R. *A line is formed diagonally across the stage from up* L *to down* R *and some of the items in the song are handed over the wall, passed down the line and off* R.

ISLAND MAN.   Ready ?
ALL.   Ready ?
ISLAND MAN.   Ready ?
ALL.   Ready.
                 The boat's in !
                 What's the boat brought in ?
                 A sack of flour
                 And a lady.
                 The boat's in
                 With the paraffin
                 And a rolling pin
                 And a lady.

MEN.	A bottle of ink	MUSIC
	And a kitchen sink	
GIRLS.	A case of wine	
	And a ball of twine	
ALL.	A cutter for the ditches	
	And a pair of leather breeches	
	And a lady	
	And a lady, lady, lady, lady, lady.	
	The boat's in.	
	What's the boat brought in?	
	A frying-pan	
	And a lady.	
	The boat's in	
	With a baking tin	
	And a tarpaulin	
	And a lady.	
MEN,	A razor blade	
	And a garden spade.	
GIRLS,	A coil of rope	
	And a box of soap	
ALL,	A bottle with a stopper	
	And a hammer and a chopper	
	And a lady	
	And a lady, lady, lady,	

ALL *gradually exit except* GERALDINE *and* ALBERT, *repeating " a lady ", more and more softly until the voices fade.*

Lady, lady, lady, lady, lady, lady.
ALBERT [*shyly*] Well, shall we s-start?
GERALDINE. I'd like to stay here for a bit, first.
ALBERT. That's the b-beach.
GERALDINE. Yes.
ALBERT [*pointing*] It's the only point where a boat can put in. In the winter, if there are gales, it isn't safe even there. But the s-summers are long.
GERALDINE. My name's Geraldine. May I call you Albert?
ALBERT. Would that be correct?
GERALDINE. No. Only fashionable.
ALBERT. Oh. [*He laughs a little shyly, moves and sits beside Geraldine on the boat*] Excuse me, Geraldine, as my uncle's nephew I'm heir to the island and I hope you'll be happy.
GERALDINE. Thank you. Do you go away with Lord Paul to seek improvements?
ALBERT. Oh, heavens, no! He never brings back improvements, he only brings—well . . .
GERALDINE. Problems.
ALBERT. Exactly. He fusses, you know. Do you happen to take the *Geographical Magazine*?
GERALDINE. Not regularly.
ALBERT. No. Well, he got very upset over breakfast. It mentioned Terhou—and do you know what it said we were?
GERALDINE. What?
ALBERT. Uninhabited.
GERALDINE [*laughing*] But why worry? He knows you're *not* uninhabited.
ALBERT. Yes, but he minds dreadfully that the *Geographical Magazine* thinks we are. He's afraid we're behind the times.
GERALDINE. Teach me about tomorrow. Is the Coronation a difficult ceremony?
ALBERT. No—there's only one thing you have to do.
GERALDINE. Yes?
ALBERT. After you're crowned, you, as the Queen, lead the people all over the island.
GERALDINE. Heavens!

ALBERT. It's quite simple: just go where you like and we'll follow. Some of the girls have led us quite a dance. *MUSIC*
GERALDINE. Is that to assert your right of possession?
ALBERT. Exactly. And there's a song we always sing . . .
GERALDINE. A patriotic song?
ALBERT. Ye-es. An expression of freedom.
GERALDINE. A bit solemn—like *Land of Hope and Glory* or *The Dam Busters' March*?
ALBERT. It's a solemn occasion. Perhaps you'd better learn it.
GERALDINE. Perhaps I had.
ALBERT [*rising and moving* RC] It goes like this.

"FREE TO SING" No. 6
ALBERT and GERALDINE

ALBERT.   North! *Bong!* South! *Bong!*
            East! *Bong!* West! *Bong!*
            Sing to the East. *Bong!*
            Sing to the West.
            When the sun's going down, we still won't rest,
            We'll drink and laugh and feast, *Bong! Bong!*
            Till the sun rises in the East.

The music stops.

GERALDINE [*rising and moving to Albert*] Albert, excuse me, but what's that "bong-bong"?
ALBERT. It's the drum. Mutch plays it.
GERALDINE. Oh. Can I put in the "bongs"?
ALBERT. Yes, do. I'll start again.

The music recommences.

ALBERT.   North!
GERALDINE. *Bong!*
ALBERT.   South!
GERALDINE. *Bong!*
ALBERT.   East!
GERALDINE. *Bong!*
ALBERT.   West!
GERALDINE. *Bong!*
ALBERT.   Sing to the East,
GERALDINE. *Bong!*
ALBERT.   Sing to the West,
GERALDINE. *Bong!*

The music stops.

ALBERT. No "bong" there. I have to go straight on.
GERALDINE. Sorry.

The music recommences.

ALBERT.   Sing to the East,
GERALDINE. *Bong!*
ALBERT.   Sing to the West
            When the sun's going down, we still won't rest,
            We'll drink and laugh and feast,
GERALDINE. *Bong! Bong!*
ALBERT.   Till the sun rises in the East.
            Sing to the South

GERALDINE.	*Bong!*
ALBERT.	Sing to the North
	At the edge of the world, the songs fly forth.
	We'll sing for all we're worth,
GERALDINE.	*Bong! Bong!*
ALBERT.	At the four corners of the earth.
	Free to sing. Free to go.
	North and South and everywhere.
	Free as air—that'll cost you nothing,
	Free as air.
GERALDINE.	Bom-pa-bom-bom-bom.
ALBERT.	Free to sing. Free to play.
	Shout to tear the world in half.
	Free to laugh—ha-ha-ha-ha-ha-ha
GERALDINE.	Free to laugh.
ALBERT.	Ha-ha-ha-ha-ha
	Follow me! Follow me!
	Merrily because
BOTH.	*Bong!*
ALBERT.	Thought is free, speech is free.
	Everything is free.
BOTH.	*Bong!*
ALBERT.	Free to sing, free to sing.
	Sing a song of anything.
	Free to sing
GERALDINE.	La-la-la-la-la-la
ALBERT.	Free to sing
BOTH.	La-la-la-la-la.
GERALDINE.	Free to sing
ALBERT.	Free to go,
BOTH.	East and West and all about.
GERALDINE.	Free to shout,
ALBERT.	Yip-py-yip-ay-ad-dy.
GERALDINE.	Free to shout,
ALBERT.	Yip-py-yip-ay-dee.
GERALDINE.	Free to sing,
ALBERT.	Free to live,
BOTH.	Spin the wheel and take your chance.
GERALDINE.	Free to dance.
ALBERT.	Tcha-tcha-tcha-tcha-tcha-tcha.
GERALDINE.	Free to dance,
ALBERT.	With a Quick Quick Slow.
BOTH.	Play some more. Shore to shore.
	Weep no more because—
	Bong!
	Love is free, beer is free,
	Everything is free—
	Bong!

	Free to sing,
	Free to sing,
	Sing a song of anything.
GERALDINE.	Free to sing,
ALBERT.	La-la-la-la-la-la
	Free to sing,
GERALDINE.	La-la-la-la-la-la-la
ALBERT.	Free to sing
GERALDINE.	La-la-la-la-la-la-la
	La-la-la-la-la-la-la-la
	Free to sing,
ALBERT.	La-la-la-la-la-la,
	Bong! Bong!
GERALDINE.	Free to sing.
ALBERT.	La-la-la-la-la-la,
	Bong! Bong!
GERALDINE.	Free as air.
ALBERT.	La-la-la-la-la-la-la-la
	La-la-la-la-la-la-la
	La-la-la-la-la-la-la
BOTH.	Bong!

EXIT MUSIC   No. 6a

GERALDINE *and* ALBERT *exit as—*

the FRONT CLOTH *falls*

SCENE 4

A Shore Front Cloth. Later the same morning.

As the music continues, BINDWEED *enters* L, *pushing* MOLLY *in a wheelbarrow.* BINDWEED, *farmer and gardener, is stout, elderly and gleefully morbid.* GREGORY, *his assistant, follows them on. He is a lanky, enthusiastic youth, much impressed by Bindweed. He carries two stools and a garland of flowers they are making for the island Queen.* MOLLY'S *lap is full of flowers.* BINDWEED *and* GREGORY *sit* C, *on the stools.*

The music fades.

GREGORY. The new lady certainly will make a beautiful Queen, won't she, Mr Bindweed?
BINDWEED. I'm not saying she's not beautiful, Mr Gregory.
GREGORY. It's a pleasure to make a garland for her. Have you got any more daisies there, Molly?
MOLLY. There's only one left. [*She hands a daisy to Gregory*]
GREGORY. Thanks very much. She must be a Prime Minister's daughter at least.
BINDWEED. Oh, she's got breeding, Mr Gregory. I'll give you that.
GREGORY. Thanks, Mr Bindweed.
MOLLY. But if you ask me, she's a disturbing influence.
GREGORY. Really?
MOLLY. Really! Oh, nothing ever disturbs you.
GREGORY. What's the matter with you, Molly? You were quite happy earlier this morning.
BINDWEED [*chanting, to tease her*] Moody Molly's melancholy.
MOLLY. Oh, shut up!
BINDWEED [*rising*] Come out of my barrow. [*He yanks Molly from the barrow*] And go and pick some more daisies.
MOLLY [*moving* L] I don't feel like it.
BINDWEED. What you need, my girl, is a husband to keep you busy.
MOLLY [*sighing rapturously*] I'd keep *him* busy.

BINDWEED. She should settle for you, Mr Gregory. She won't do better.
GREGORY [sadly] Oh, I don't know.
MOLLY [having read it somewhere] Marriage is a very big step in a girl's life.
BINDWEED. Nothing like a husband for taking your mind off it. [He indicates the garland] Slip it on, Mr Gregory, will you?

GREGORY rises. BINDWEED puts the garland around Gregory's neck.

GREGORY. Do you like it, Molly?
MOLLY. She'd look all right in anything.
GREGORY. What's the matter with you today?
MOLLY. It's her. [She crosses to Bindweed] She's what's the matter.
GREGORY. The new lady?
MOLLY. She's so beautiful.
GREGORY. What's the harm in that, Molly?
MOLLY. Well, if she's as beautiful as that, just think what the *men* must be like.
GREGORY. What must they be like?
MOLLY. Oh, you don't understand at all.
GREGORY. You're not yourself today, Molly.

"A MAN FROM THE MAINLAND" No. 7

MOLLY

MOLLY [over the music] Nor would you be, if you were me. [She crosses to RC, kneels and sings]

Why am I so restless?
Why do I gaze and gaze
At a land I cannot even see,
Hoping that happiness happens to me
One of these lazy days?
[She rises and moves C]

I want a man from the mainland,
I am wilting rather sadly,
For I'm certain that another land
Is the land for me.
I do want a man from the mainland,
And I want him pretty badly
To remove me to the motherland
Of the brave and free.
[She moves down L]

Take me away
Over the Channel,
Where nobody sleeps
In calico or flannel.
Hurry! Hurry!
Oh, I do want a man from the mainland,
I am pining for him madly,
To escort me to that other land
Far across the sea.
[She moves to the barrow and sits]

Here am I imploring,
Nobody seems to hear.

BINDWEED. I am keen to live and keen to learn;
I want a bath with a tap I can turn.
When will my man appear?
When will her man appear?

MOLLY rises and dances with BINDWEED.

MOLLY. I want a man from the mainland,
Very handsome, very witty.
Who will pluck at mandolines with me
In a coffee bar.

[*She breaks from Bindweed and moves above the barrow*]

I do want a man from the mainland,
Spick and spansome, from the city,
Who will go for little spins with me
In a horseless car.

[*She moves down* L]

Take me away
Past the horizon
And buy me a skirt
With little hooks and eyes on.
Hurry! Hurry!

GREGORY and BINDWEED pick Molly up and swing her.

Oh! I do want a man from the mainland,
Where the menfolk are so pretty,
To remove me from this plain land,

GREGORY and BINDWEED put Molly down.

To the sacred and profane land
For I'm certain that the mainland
Is the land for me.
[*She sits in the barrow*]

BINDWEED *wheels* MOLLY *off* R. GREGORY *follows them off, taking the stools with him.*

SCENE 5

Exterior of Shop and Miss Catamole's Cottage.

The afternoon of the same day.

Miss Catamole's cottage is R. *In front of it there is a bench and a table. Mr Mutch's shop, with a gay canopy, is* L. *In front of the shop there are two stools with a beer barrel between them for use as a table.* ALBERT *and* GERALDINE *enter up* L *on the rostrum and come down* C. *They have been running and are breathless.*

ALBERT [*pointing*] That's the highest point; it's over three hundred and fifty feet. [*He points to the shop* L] This is the shop. Would you like me to buy you some beer?
GERALDINE. Beer?
ALBERT [*crossing to the shop*] Or there's—whisky—rum—ginger-beer . . .
GERALDINE. At four o'clock in the afternoon?
ALBERT. Isn't that customary in London?
GERALDINE. It isn't legal.

ALBERT *looks puzzled.*

Thank you, Albert, I'd like some beer.

ALBERT [*calling*] Mutch! [*He peers into the shop*] Oh, he isn't here. [*He reaches into the shop and brings out a bottle of beer and two glasses*] Will this do?
GERALDINE *nods*. ALBERT *puts the glasses on the barrel and pours out the beer.*
GERALDINE [*looking off up* R *and shading her eyes*] Can you see the other islands from up there?
ALBERT. Sometimes. When it's exceptionally clear.
GERALDINE. Jersey?
ALBERT. Just.
GERALDINE [*moving to the stool* R *of the barrel*] Then they can see us. [*She sits*]
ALBERT *sits* L *of the barrel.*
[*She picks up her drink*] Thank you. Cheers!
ALBERT. I beg your pardon?
GERALDINE [*absently*] It's a custom. You raise your glass and say something heartening. It makes drinking jolly.
ALBERT. Drinking's jolly anyway.
GERALDINE. Does everyone guess that I've run away?
ALBERT. Is it from the police?
GERALDINE. No. There are two things: one of them's a racing motorist who wants to marry me, and when I say "no", he just thinks I'm playing hard-to-get.
ALBERT. Playing what?
GERALDINE. Oh, dear, you won't understand the other thing, either. It's the Press. I'm famous. All over England babies and cigarettes are being christened after me.
ALBERT *looks blank*. GERALDINE *laughs at Albert's blank face.*
ALBERT. Really? Why?
GERALDINE. I've been left half a million pounds.
ALBERT [*unimpressed*] Oh.
GERALDINE. Oh, dear, you don't understand. It was left me by a relation I didn't know I had, and when something like that happens, London falls in on top of you. You see, the Press adopt you—and within three months you're the intimate friend of the entire British Isles.
ALBERT. Except Terhou.
GERALDINE [*copying his inflection*] Exactly!

They laugh.

ALBERT. Couldn't you stop them?
GERALDINE. Oh, I tried. But it only made new headlines. I ran away three times. The last time it was Jersey.
ALBERT. And they caught you?
GERALDINE. Jack Amersham gave me away.
ALBERT. Is he the racing motorist you wants to marry you?
GERALDINE. Yes. After that a reporter girl from the *Daily Echo* turned up. She was quite young, quite pretty and quite ruthless. Her name was Ivy Crush. Wherever we went, she was there—always there—asking questions and providing the answers. This morning I'd had enough. I went down to the beach and found a boatman who'd never even heard of me. Oh, Albert, promise me you'll never ask me who are the men in my life.
ALBERT. Won't Mr Amersham be wondering where you are?
GERALDINE. I don't expect so. [*She pauses*] What are you thinking?
ALBERT. Tell me some more heartening things you say before drinking.
GERALDINE. "Here's looking at you."
ALBERT. How very curious. "Here's looking at you."

MOLLY, MISS CATAMOLE, BINDWEED, GREGORY, TOM *and the* ISLAND MEN *and* GIRLS *enter in twos and threes from different directions. They stand around Geraldine, staring and grinning. They are conspiratorial and happy.*

GERALDINE [*to the first group*] Hullo!

The ISLANDERS *smile and nod.*

[*To the second group*] Good afternoon.

The ISLANDERS *smile and nod.*

Can I buy you all a drink?

The ISLANDERS *shake their heads. A* GIRL *laughs.*

Well [*she raises her glass; nervously*] here's looking at you. [*She drinks*]

LORD PAUL *and* MUTCH *enter happily and swiftly up* R *and cross to* C. LORD PAUL *carries his megaphone.*

MUTCH. Here we are, then! Here we are! Are we all met? Miss Melford . . .

GERALDINE *rises and moves down* LC.

LORD PAUL [*butting in*] Miss Melford, we're happy to tell you that we've made a new law. All it requires is my signature. Where is the law, Mutch?
MUTCH. I thought *you* had it. [*He looks around and calls*] Potter!
LORD PAUL [*calling through his megaphone*] Potter!
ALL. Potter!

POTTER *enters busily up* L, *as if he has not heard. He carries a document, a bottle of ink and a pen.*

POTTER [*crossing to* C] Here we are, then. Are we all met? Miss Melford, we're happy to tell you that we've made a new law. All it requires is Lord Paul's signature. [*He holds out the document*] Lord Paul.

The ISLANDERS *gather round as* LORD PAUL *signs the document.*

LORD PAUL. Miss Melfold, you are now—
MUTCH. —in everything except fact—
POTTER. —a native of Terhou.

The ISLANDERS *clap.*

GERALDINE. Thank you very much.
LORD PAUL [*taking a small box from his pocket*] I now have great pleasure in presenting you with the freedom of the island.

The ISLANDERS *clap.* GERALDINE *moves to* L *of* LORD PAUL *who hands her the box.*

GERALDINE. Oh. Can I open it now? [*She opens the box and takes out a miniature turtle on a chain*] It's a turtle. Oh, thank you.
LORD PAUL. May I have the honour? [*He clasps the chain around her neck*] There!
GERALDINE. Oh, thank you. Thank you.
LORD PAUL. Excuse me, but there's a song we all sing after the Coronation.
GERALDINE. Yes. I've learnt it.
POTTER. Oh, let's do it. Let's do it *now*.
LORD PAUL. Is the band ready?
MUTCH. I'm not playing my drum till the day.
MOLLY. Oh, go on, Mr Mutch.
MUTCH. No. Not till tomorrow.
MOLLY. Oh, don't, then.
MUTCH. All right.

SCENE 5 — FREE AS AIR

REPRISE
"FREE TO SING"

ENSEMBLE

At the beginning of the number one of the ISLAND MEN *gets* MUTCH's *drum and gleefully plays it until* MUTCH *jealously snatches it and plays it himself.*

MUTCH.	North!
ALL.	*Bong!*
MUTCH.	South!
ALL.	*Bong!*
MUTCH.	East!
ALL.	*Bong!*
MUTCH.	West!
ALL.	*Bong!*
MUTCH.	Sing to the East! *Bong!*
ALL.	Sing to the West! When the sun's going down we still won't rest, We'll drink and laugh and feast. *Bong! Bong!* Till the sun rises in the East.
MUTCH.	Sing to the South! *Bong!*
ALL.	Sing to the North! At the edge of the world the songs fly forth. We'll sing for all we're worth, *Bong! Bong!* At the four corners of the earth.
GERALDINE.	Free to sing.
ALL.	Free to go, North and South and everywhere.
GERALDINE.	Free as air That'll cost you nothing, Free as air, Bom-pa-bom-bom-bom. Free to sing.
ALL.	Free to play! Shout to tear the world in half. Free to laugh, Ha-ha-ha-ha-ha-ha! Free to laugh, Ha-ha-ha-ha-ha!
GERALDINE.	Follow me, follow me, merrily because, *Bong!*
ALL.	Thought is free, Speech is free, Everything is free. *Bong!* Free to sing, free to sing, Sing a song of anything. Free to sing, La-la-la-la-la-la. Free to sing, La-la-la-la-la.

GIRLS.	Everybody is allowed to be shouting, Allowed to be shouting loud as he can. Free to sing all over the island, Free to sing loud as he can. Everybody is allowed to be laughing, Allowed to be laughing loud as he can. Free to shout all over the island, Free to shout loud as he can.		
MUTCH.	Follow everybody hand in hand Over the rocks and over the sand.		
ISLAND MAN.	Follow ev'rybody single file, Follow the Queen For mile after mile after mile after mile after mile.		
ALL.	Follow the Queen. Ev'rybody is allowed to be singing, Allowed to be singing loud as he can. Free to sing all over the island Free to sing loud as he can.		
GIRLS.	Everybody is allowed to be shouting Allowed to be shouting Loud as he can	MEN.	Free to sing Free to go East and West and all about
	Free to shout all over the island Free to shout loud as he can! Everybody is allowed to be laughing Allowed to be laughing Loud as he can		Free to sing. Free to shout! Free to sing Free to live Spin the wheel and take your chance
	Free to laugh all over the island Free to laugh loud as he can!		Free to dance Free to dance
ALL.	Play some more, shore to shore, Weep no more because, *Bong!* Love is free, beer is free, Everything is free, *Bong!* Free to sing, free to sing, Sing a song of anything.		
GIRLS. MEN.	Free to sing. La-la-la-la-la-la-la! Free to sing.		
GIRLS. MEN. GIRLS.	La-la-la-la-la-la-la! Free to sing La-la-la-la-la-la-la, La-la-la-la-la-la-la,		
ALL. GIRLS. MEN.	La-la. Free to sing. La-la-la-la,		

ALL.	La-la.			
GIRLS.	Free to sing.			
MEN.	La-la-la-la,			
ALL.	La-la.			
GIRLS.	Free to sing.		MEN.	La-la-la-la-la
				La-la-la-la-la
				La-la-la-la-la
				La-la-la-la-la-la,
				To sing.
ALL [*spoken*]	Bong!			

EXIT MUSIC No. 9

At the end of the number, GERALDINE *is led ceremoniously into Miss Catamole's house.* MISS CATAMOLE *follows. Two* ISLAND MEN *move the bench* R *to face front* RC, *and put the table behind it. An* ISLAND GIRL *gets a cider-flagon and two cups from Miss Catamole's house and puts them on the table.* ALL *exit except* ALBERT. LORD PAUL *is the last to go.* ALBERT *moves* RC *and looks at Miss Catamole's house, then calls to Lord Paul.*

ALBERT [*calling*] Uncle Paul!
LORD PAUL [*stopping and turning*] What is it, Albert?
ALBERT. Can I have a word with you? [*He glances rather proudly at Miss Catamole's house*] I've got a problem, actually.
LORD PAUL [*moving to* L *of Albert*] You want some advice?
ALBERT. No, I want to give you some. Suppose I ever wanted to get m-married, who would look after you?
LORD PAUL. Heavens above! Can't I look after myself?
ALBERT. Oh, n-not possibly! I'm your cook, valet, housemaid and nursemaid. So you need a wife.
LORD PAUL. A wife? [*Reasonably*] Well, do you think I haven't known that for years? I can't find any woman as nice as my mother.
ALBERT. There's Miss Catamole. She's a very motherly lady.
LORD PAUL. Mm! She is motherly, Albert, but is she beautiful?
ALBERT. She has a great admiration for you.
LORD PAUL. Oh? Well, perhaps she is a *bit* beautiful.

LORD PAUL *and* ALBERT *stroll off up* L, *talking.*

GERALDINE *enters from Miss Catamole's house. She carries a large hat and a mirror.*

GERALDINE [*calling into the house; delighted*] You look quite beautiful, Miss Catamole. Come out. There isn't room in there.

MISS CATAMOLE *enters from her house. She is wearing a long skirt and a stole.*

MISS CATAMOLE [*laughing*] Oh! Ha, ha, ha! Well, I never did in all my life!
GERALDINE [*arranging the stole*] Try it this way.
MISS CATAMOLE. Oh, Miss Melford, your beautiful things.
GERALDINE. Try the hat, too.
MISS CATAMOLE. Oh! [*She takes the hat and puts it on*] It's only in fun, of course.
GERALDINE. It suits you. Look. [*She holds up the mirror*]
MISS CATAMOLE [*looking in the mirror*] Ha, ha, ha, ha! It hides my face, that's an improvement.
GERALDINE. Why have you never married, Miss Catamole?
MISS CATAMOLE [*arranging the hat*] Mr Potter never asked me.
GERALDINE. You're fond of him?
MISS CATAMOLE. Oh, very.

GERALDINE. And is he fond of you? MUSIC
MISS CATAMOLE. Oh, very. But men are so lazy, aren't they?
GERALDINE. Perhaps he only needs to see you looking different. [*She glances* L] Sh! Here he is.

POTTER enters up L.

POTTER. Oh, I beg your pardon, I was looking for Miss Catamole.

POTTER *exits into the shop* L. GERALDINE *and* MISS CATAMOLE *laugh and embrace.*

MISS CATAMOLE. There! I'm looking *too* different.
GERALDINE. Never mind. [*She puts the mirror on the table* RC]

LORD PAUL *and* ALBERT *enter up* L *and cross to* C.

ALBERT [*urgently*] Geraldine . . .
LORD PAUL [*looking at Miss Catamole; awestruck*] Miss Catamole!
ALBERT [*to Geraldine*] Will you come with me? I want to—er—show you the beach.
GERALDINE. But I've seen the beach.
ALBERT. No. This is another beach.

ALBERT *and* GERALDINE *exit up* L. MISS CATAMOLE *moves to the table* RC.

LORD PAUL [*admiringly*] Miss Catamole! Is this really you?
MISS CATAMOLE [*picking up a cup and polishing it on the stole*] Mr Potter didn't think so.
LORD PAUL [*gallantly*] It *can't* be.
MISS CATAMOLE. No, I don't think it can.
LORD PAUL. You must have known. That I was coming to see you on a romantic mission.

MISS CATAMOLE *breathes loudly on to the cup.*

MISS CATAMOLE. On a what?
LORD PAUL [*moving close to her*] Albert's been telling me things. Lots of things.

MISS CATAMOLE *turns smartly to Lord Paul and the brim of her hat strikes him.*

MISS CATAMOLE. Doesn't he usually tell you things?
LORD PAUL. Other things but not these things.
MISS CATAMOLE. Will you have some dandelion wine?
LORD PAUL. You even prepared the wine.
MISS CATAMOLE [*pouring two cups of wine*] Don't I always for the Coronation? [*She hands a cup to Lord Paul*] Taste it. [*She takes her cup and sits on the bench* RC, *at the right end*]
LORD PAUL [*sitting* L *of Miss Catamole on the bench*] I'm honoured. [*He raises his cup*] Dear Miss Catamole, your health. [*He drinks*]
MISS CATAMOLE [*raising her cup*] Mud in your eye. [*She drinks*]
LORD PAUL [*spluttering*] Good heavens! What on earth . . . ?
MISS CATAMOLE. Miss Melford taught it me. It's a compliment, really.
LORD PAUL [*choking slightly*] It's a little difficult to swallow. I think a pipe would soothe me. Have you any objection?
MISS CATAMOLE. None at all. [*She puts her cup on the table*]

LORD PAUL *puts his cup on the table and takes his recorder from his pocket.*

LORD PAUL. Do you remember when *you* were Queen at the Coronation, Miss Catamole? All those years ago.
MISS CATAMOLE [*rising and moving to the house door* R] Distinctly.
LORD PAUL. And the tune I played on that day?
MISS CATAMOLE. The one you've been playing ever since?
LORD PAUL [*gravely*] To change it, Miss Catamole, would be to rewrite the National Anthem. [*He rises, faces* L *and plays*]

MISS CATAMOLE *exits quietly into her house.*

SCENE 5   FREE AS AIR

[*He breaks off and speaks without turning*] How quiet it is, Miss Catamole, I suddenly feel a lonely man. Albert intimated just now that you may not be without regard for me. In a flash, I saw how badly I needed a wife. All my restlessness—my leaving the island—my sudden desperate urges to go to Jersey. If I had *you* instead . . . Miss Catamole, will you be my Jersey—to knit and to purl from this day forward? Will you marry me? [*He pauses*] I know it must come as a shock: don't hurry with your reply. [*He pauses*] Take your time. [*He pauses*] Within reason, of course. [*He turns and sees she has gone*] Miss Catamole!

                         MISS CATAMOLE *enters from her house, carrying her knitting.*

MISS CATAMOLE. Yes?
LORD PAUL. Did you hear what I was saying? [*He puts his recorder in his pocket*]
MISS CATAMOLE. No. Was it important? [*She sits on the bench at the right end*]
LORD PAUL. Was it . . . ? [*He recovers a little*] It was something very close to my heart. [*He picks up his cup and raises it*] Miss Catamole . . .
MISS CATAMOLE. Down the hatch! [*She counts stitches*]
LORD PAUL [*sitting L of her on the bench*] I came here this evening because there's something very . . .
MISS CATAMOLE. . . . sixty-six, sixty-seven, sixty-eight, sixty-nine, seventy. Go on.
LORD PAUL. Seventy-one, seventy-two, seventy-three, seventy-four . . .
MISS CATAMOLE. No, go on with what you were saying.
LORD PAUL [*putting his cup on the table*] If I thought I had your attention . . .
MISS CATAMOLE. You have my full attention. [*She takes a skein of wool from her bag*]
LORD PAUL. Then, Miss Catamole, I came here . . .

                        As LORD PAUL *stretches out his hands to give emphasis to his words,*
                        MISS CATAMOLE *pops the wool on to them and starts winding.*

MISS CATAMOLE. Do you mind?
LORD PAUL. Very happy. I wanted to ask . . . [*He tries to stop a sneeze with a finger and searches for a handkerchief, still holding the wool*] I wanted to ask—I wanted to ask you to marry me. [*The sneeze comes in time to obliterate the word* " *marry* "]
MISS CATAMOLE. Bless you!

                        LORD PAUL *continues to search for his handkerchief.* MISS
                        CATAMOLE *continues to wind the wool. Finally, he puts his feet*
                        up on the bench, puts the wool on them and finds his handkerchief.

LORD PAUL [*wiping his nose*] Albert gave me some wise advice just now. Are you listening?
MISS CATAMOLE. Of course.
LORD PAUL. You seem to me to be wool-gathering. Shall I go on?
MISS CATAMOLE [*finishing the winding*] That's enough for the moment. You were saying?
LORD PAUL [*putting his feet to the ground*] Albert said something about our future together.
MISS CATAMOLE [*taking the pieces of her knitting from the bag*] Yours and Albert's? Did you take his advice? [*She holds the front of a sweater against him to fit it*]
LORD PAUL. I'm trying to. But it's very difficult.

                        MISS CATAMOLE *fits the back and front pieces of the sweater.*

MISS CATAMOLE. You were saying about your future with Albert.
LORD PAUL. No. There's something I want to ask . . .
MISS CATAMOLE [*rising*] Do you mind? [*She rises his arm to a horizontal position to fit the sleeve*]
LORD PAUL. Something very close to my . . .
MISS CATAMOLE. Bend, please.
LORD PAUL [*bending forward*] Something very close to my bend.
MISS CATAMOLE. Elbow.
LORD PAUL. To my elbow.
MISS CATAMOLE. I meant bend your elbow, please.

                        LORD PAUL *bends his elbow with his body still bent.*

LORD PAUL. Something very close to my heart, which has been bothering me for some years.
MISS CATAMOLE. Higher.

LORD PAUL [*in a high-pitched voice*] Which has been bothering me for some years. MUSIC
MISS CATAMOLE. No. Your arm higher. [*She raises Lord Paul's arm to measure the inside arm*]
LORD PAUL [*barely audible because of his bent position*] Miss Catamole, I didn't think I would ever find myself in a position like this.

        MISS CATAMOLE *finishes her fitting and puts her knitting on the table.*

I believe it's time I came down to earth.

        MISS CATAMOLE *picks up her drink.*

Living all alone up there at the Big House, alone except for Albert, of course . .
MISS CATAMOLE [*raising her cup*] Bottoms up! [*She sips her drink*]

        LORD PAUL *raises his bottom from the bench.*

LORD PAUL. You, with your busy life and your humble surroundings, and your beautiful nature . . .

        MISS CATAMOLE *notices* LORD PAUL'S *position.*

MISS CATAMOLE. Looking for something?
LORD PAUL [*passionately*] I'm looking for *you*, Miss Catamole.
MISS CATAMOLE [*tapping his shoulder*] Here I am.
LORD PAUL [*straightening up*] Excuse me, I feel a little dizzy. [*He sits on the bench*]
MISS CATAMOLE. Have some wine.
LORD PAUL. Thank you. Your . . .
MISS CATAMOLE [*raising her cup*] Happy hunting! [*She drinks*] What did you say you'd lost?
LORD PAUL [*exhausted*] Heart.
MISS CATAMOLE. Don't lose heart. I know what it is. You think Albert may want to marry Miss Melfold. Well, you must get a wife of your own.
LORD PAUL [*embracing Miss Catamole's knees*] At last!
MISS CATAMOLE. What are you doing? Let me go! Lord Paul!
LORD PAUL. Will you marry me?
MISS CATAMOLE. Of course not.
LORD PAUL. I love you.
MISS CATAMOLE. You do nothing of the sort.
LORD PAUL. Don't I?
MISS CATAMOLE [*laughing*] No, of course not.
LORD PAUL [*terrified*] Oh, but Albert said . . . [*He stuffs the end of Miss Catamole's stole into his breast pocket and rises*] Miss Catamole, on my knees, I implore you.

        LORD PAUL *drops to his knees, clutches Miss Catamole round her waist and pulls down her long skirt.*

        HURRY MUSIC   No. 10

        MISS CATAMOLE *is wearing her usual skirt under the long one* LORD PAUL *does not realize this, rises and exits hurriedly* L *as—*

        the FRONT CLOTH *falls*

        The MUSIC *continues.*

SCENE 6

The Shore Front Cloth. Early the same evening.

LORD PAUL *enters* L. *He is haggard and incoherent, and wears oilskins and a sou'wester.*

        The MUSIC *fades.*

LORD PAUL [*crossing to* C] Oh, heavens! Oh, gracious heavens! What will become of me? [*He

SCENE 6   FREE AS AIR

mops his brow] Women! Snakes! Dragons! Never head up my hold again. [*He consults his watch*] What tide is it? What tide's the time? Women! Oh, prosex me from the opposite tect. Six-thirty.   MUSIC

                           ALBERT *and* GERALDINE, *unseen by* LORD PAUL, *enter down* R *and cross to* R *of him.*

Protex me from the opposite . . . [*He turns and sees Albert*]   Aaaaaaah!
ALBERT. What's the matter, Uncle Paul?
LORD PAUL. Nothing at all. Nothing. [*He shakes hands with them both*] Good evening, Miss—er . . . Just that I fool rather a feel. [*He crosses down* RC] Excuse me. Must get on. It's tide for the time.
ALBERT. Uncle Paul!
LORD PAUL. Sorry! Just on sex-thirty. I must go down—to the seas again. Good-bye.

                           LORD PAUL *exits* R.

GERALDINE. Is he going to drown himself?
ALBERT. No. He's often like that. Now he'll go running off to the mainland. He always does when he's in difficulties.
GERALDINE. You disapprove of that.
ALBERT. A bit.
GERALDINE. Then you disapprove of me, because I've run away.
ALBERT [*touching her shoulder*] Never mind. You'll be s-safe here. You like Terhou, Geraldine?
GERALDINE. Yes. I find it suits me—thank you.

                               REPRISE   No. 11

                       "NOTHING BUT SEA AND SKY"

                           GERALDINE and ALBERT

GERALDINE.	Shimmering sky
	Over a gentle sea.
BOTH.	We're on our own
	And glad to be
	Where there is
	Nothing but sea and sky
GERALDINE.	And the world so still that I
	Only hear the water whispering peace to me.
	I can hear the waves
	And echoing caves
	Telling me I'm alone
BOTH.	and free

                      GERALDINE *and* ALBERT *exit* L *as—*

                      the LIGHTS BLACK-OUT

Scene 7

The Bar of the Octopus Hotel, Jersey. Later the same evening

The bar itself is in the corner up R, with shelves behind for bottles, glasses, etc. The entrance is through an arch up L. Four high stools stand at the bar and there is a small table and chair down L. A telephone stands on the downstage corner of the bar counter.

"DAILY ECHO" No. 11a
Ivy and Ensemble

When the Front Cloth *rises,* François, *the barman, is behind the bar. He is dressed as a Breton.* Ivy Crush *enters up* C, *carrying two suitcases. She crosses, puts the cases on the floor down* R, *goes to the telephone and lifts the receiver.*

Ivy [*singing into the telephone*]
Operator, operator, operator, operator.
Will you get me Fleet Street
One-seven-three-four ?
Get it, quickly, be a sport.
What's my number ? Jersey-nought.
[*She pauses and swings the receiver*]
Daily Echo ? This is Ivy Crush on the line.
Can you hear me ? Could we have some hush on the line ?

The following lines are spoken in time with the music.

Jack Amersham wins race
Grand Prix for handsome ace.
Hot candidate for Geraldine's hand
Rides to triumph on the sand.
Hold everything. Tell the Ed
To keep a great big double-page spread
There's a red-hot scoop coming in with the tide
Of the Jersey winner and his heiress bride.
'Bye for now. I'll give you a ring.
Don't worry, I won't miss a thing.
[*She replaces the receiver*]
Large Scotch, please, waiter !
See you later, operator !

The Music *continues.*

Six Girls *and two* Mechanics *enter chattering excitedly up* L. Ivy *crosses and sits on the chair down* L.

Jack Amersham *enters up* L *and leaps on to the shoulders of the* Mechanics. *He wears goggles on his forehead and a garland around his neck.*

Jack [*singing*] I've done it again !
Girls [*shouting over the music*]
Bravo, Jack ! Bravo, Jack !
Jack [*singing*] I've won it again !
Girls [*shouting over the music*]
Bravo, Jack ! Bravo, Jack !
Who's the hero of today ?

The Mechanics *turn and set* Jack *on the bar.*

J A C K !

SCENE 7 FREE AS AIR

JACK. Drinks all round, Franco. Large Scotch for me. [*He jumps from the bar and moves* c] Now, where's Geraldine?
IVY. What do you mean—where's Geraldine?
JACK. I'm asking you.
IVY. Wasn't she at the race?

FRANÇOIS *puts a tray on the counter with nine whiskies. A MECHANIC hands a drink to Jack. The others help themselves.*

JACK. Of course not. Isn't she in the hotel?
IVY. No.
JACK. Then where . . . ? [*He turns to the bar*] Franco, where's Miss Melford?
FRANÇOIS. Gone, Mr Amersham.
JACK. Gone!
IVY. What do you mean?
FRANÇOIS. Early this morning. Paid her bill and took her luggage.
IVY [*rising and crossing to Jack*] But where's she gone?
JACK. She must have left a message?
FRANÇOIS. No, she didn't say anything.
JACK. So she's run out on me.
IVY. And me!
JACK. You! Clinging Ivy. I didn't think you'd let her escape.
IVY. Don't! Don't!
JACK. What will the *Daily Echo* say, Ivy?
IVY [*moving down* L *and sitting*] I shall be sacked. They told me to be Geraldine's little shadow.
JACK. No wonder she bolted. It was obviously to get away from you.
IVY [*suddenly standing up to him*] Or you!
JACK. Why on earth should she want to get away from me?
A GIRL [*dryly*] It's happened before, you know.
JACK. Yes, I know it happened with you—but it was your mother's fault. It's not the girls who think I won't do. It's the mothers. I can't imagine what they've got against me.

"HER MUMMY DOESN'T LIKE ME ANY MORE" No. 12

JACK and CHORUS

JACK.
In the hope of going steady
I've a ring that I keep ready,
Ready for any girl who comes along.
It appears each time like Jack-in-the-box
But it always ends up back in the box
Why is it my romances all go wrong?

Girls have got me under their skin
And I've got girls under my thumb,
Till somebody else comes butting in
And who's that somebody?

ALL [*spoken*] Mum!

CHORUS. She removes those girls from under your thumb.
JACK.
Sally was the first girl,
Her mummy thought me twee,
She sent an invitation with a huge R.S.V.P.
I went without replying, bringing twenty friends with me.
Her mummy doesn't like me any more.
CHORUS. She doesn't like you.

JACK.	Then I rang up Angie. I said, "Oh, mistress mine, I've booked a room at Brighton, Let's hope the weather's fine." The telephone exploded. It was mummy on the line. Her mummy doesn't like me any more.	MUSIC
CHORUS.	She doesn't like you.	
JACK.	Why doesn't mummy like me? Her progeny can't resist, But sooner or later The angry mater Crosses me off her shopping list.	
	Number three was Pam'la, I took her for a spin. She longed to have a cuddle But was frightened to begin. When she went home to mother She was loaded up with gin. Her mummy doesn't like me any more.	
CHORUS.	Mummy doesn't like you, Mummy doesn't like you, Mummy doesn't like you any more.	
JACK.	Barbie was the fourth girl, I took her to a ball, I sat her in the corner, Cocooned in mummy's shawl. She looked so comfy there, I didn't dance with her at all. Her mummy doesn't like me any more.	
CHORUS.	She doesn't like you.	
JACK.	Chloe was the fifth girl, At first her mum was keen, She showed me their estate Which was down at Rottingdean. I said "You've got the biggest Country seat I've ever seen." Her mummy doesn't like me any more.	
CHORUS.	She doesn't like you.	
JACK.	Why doesn't mummy like me? I'm not such a deadly sin. But mummy tells daughter She always oughter Leap from a taxi that I am in.	
	Lucy was the sixth girl, I took her to a bar; I shouted at the barmaid "How ruddy slow you are." Then Lucy said "I'd like to Introduce you to mama." Her mummy doesn't like me any more.	

SCENE 7   FREE AS AIR

                    Geraldine's the seventh,
                    She hasn't got a mum,
                    And yet she's gone and left me,
                    Which seems a trifle rum
                    So clearly in the end
                    To this conclusion I must come
                    That no-one really likes me any more.
                    No-one really likes me
CHORUS.   No-one really likes you
JACK.   No-one really likes me any more.
CHORUS.   No-one really likes you any more.

                                      FRANÇOIS *rings his bell.*

FRANÇOIS. Mesdames et messieurs: dinner is served.
A GIRL. Dinner! Come on, I'm starved.

                                The GIRL *exits up* L.

CHORUS [*ad lib*]   Come along, darling. Dinner. Jack, come and eat.

                        ALL *except* IVY, JACK *and* FRANÇOIS *exit up* L.   IVY *moves to the
                        bar and sits on the downstage stool* R.

IVY. Don't worry, Mr Amersham. We'll find Geraldine.
JACK [*sitting on the table down* L]   But where the hell do we start?

                        LORD PAUL *enters up* L. *He wears his oilskins and carries a boat-
                        hook. He falls ravaged over the bar.*

LORD PAUL. Quick, François! A tonic!
FRANÇOIS. Tonic water, Lord Paul?
LORD PAUL. No water. Just tonic.
FRANÇOIS. Something the matter, Lord Paul?
LORD PAUL. Matter! [*He holds out his hand*] Look at that. I'm shaking like a leaf. Women! Snakes! Dragons! Aah! [*He covers his face*]
IVY [*to François*] Is it D.T.s?
LORD PAUL [*suddenly advancing on Ivy*] Young woman! If I had D.T.s it wouldn't be snakes I saw, it'd be *you.*
IVY. Me?
LORD PAUL. Oh, excuse me. Terrible state. [*He crosses to Jack and sits on the chair down* L]   Do you find you run away from women?
JACK. No, they run away from me. You haven't seen one, have you?
LORD PAUL. Yes.
JACK. Not a rather beautiful one with fair hair?
LORD PAUL. Yes.
JACK. And a lot of beautiful luggage?
JACK }
IVY } [*together*]   Yes.

                                IVY *crosses to Lord Paul.*

LORD PAUL. And a yellow dress?
JACK }
IVY } [*together*]   Yes.
LORD PAUL. She arrived this morning on the boat.
JACK }
IVY } [*together*]   Arrived where?
LORD PAUL. At home. Made me do her knitting. Asked her to marry me, and she laughed.
IVY. Lord Paul . . .
LORD PAUL. Then she took her clothes off.
IVY [*moving close to Lord Paul*] What you need is a little real sympathy.
LORD PAUL. Yes!

LORD PAUL *chases* IVY *to the bar and they sit on the stools below it.* MUSIC

IVY. And a little real drink.
JACK. Large Scotch, Franco.

FRANÇOIS *pours a whisky for Lord Paul.*

IVY. Come, tell me all your troubles.
LORD PAUL. I've run away again, and I vowed I'd give it up.
IVY. Give what up?
LORD PAUL. The mainland. And I don't even like it. It's a drug. An escape.
IVY. Never mind. Drink that up and I'll see the women don't get you.
LORD PAUL. Will you, really?
JACK [*rising and crossing to Lord Paul*] Bottoms up!
LORD PAUL. Don't say that.
IVY. Sh! Is it a beautiful island where you live?
LORD PAUL. Oh, yes. Terhou.
IVY. And you ran away.
LORD PAUL. Oh, dear!
IVY. You shouldn't have done that. I'm sure you can't be spared.
LORD PAUL. Can't I?
IVY. Of course not. Terhou needs you. [*She rises*] You'd feel very brave if you went back.

LORD PAUL *rises.* IVY *takes him by the arm and leads him down* C.

LORD PAUL. I'm beginning to feel quite brave already.
IVY. That's right. Come along, I'll see you home.
JACK. We'll both see you home.
LORD PAUL. How kind you are. How can I show my gratitude?
IVY. By taking us to your beautiful island.
JACK. In your beautiful boat.
LORD PAUL. With pleasure.

REPRISE   No. 13

"THE BOAT'S IN"

LORD PAUL, IVY and JACK

LORD PAUL.	Ready?
IVY.	Ready.

JACK *picks up Ivy's suitcases and collects a bottle of port from François.*

LORD PAUL.	Ready?
JACK and IVY.	Ready.
ALL.	The boat's in, I shall go on board
	With a racing man and a lady.

JACK *slips the bottle into Lord Paul's pocket and puts the cases, one each, under Lord Paul's arms.*

	The boat's in, you can rest assured
	I'll do all I can for a lady.
JACK.	We'll brave the brine with a rich red wine
LORD PAUL.	A glass of port makes the journey short
ALL.	For a Lord who is erratic
JACK.	And a motoring fanatic

IVY.   And a lady
ALL.   And a lady, lady, lady, lady, lady.

   JACK, LORD PAUL *and* IVY *exit up* L.
   The LIGHTS BLACK-OUT *as—*
   the FRONT CLOTH *falls*
   The MUSIC *continues.*

SCENE 8

The Shore Front Cloth. Later the same night.

IVY, LORD PAUL *and* JACK *enter* L. LORD PAUL *is carrying Ivy's suitcases.*
   The MUSIC *fades.*

LORD PAUL. Come along. This way. Just follow the path.
IVY. What a darling little island. I wouldn't have missed this for anything.
LORD PAUL. I live up there at the Big House.
IVY. How lovely. Do you rule everyone from up there?
LORD PAUL. I think I may say I have complete authority.
JACK. A sort of dictator.
LORD PAUL. Benevolent, of course.
IVY. How wonderful to have so much power.

   BINDWEED, TOM *and* MUTCH *enter* R. BINDWEED *carries a pitchfork,* TOM *an oar and* MUTCH *a lantern.*

JACK. Yes. Well, how about using some of it to get me to Geraldine?
LORD PAUL. Of course, Mr Amersham. Just follow the path.

   JACK *crosses to* RC *and is threatened by* TOM.

JACK. There seems to be some sort of opposition.
IVY. Are these some of the natives? [*She crosses to* RC]

   TOM *threatens Ivy.*

Oh, they're hostile.
LORD PAUL [*crossing below the others to Tom*] Just leave it to me. Tom, stop being hostile.

   TOM *pokes Lord Paul with the oar.*

Put down that oar. Tom!
JACK. I can see your word is law.
LORD PAUL. Bindweed, go home.
MUTCH. Lord Paul, you've done a very bad thing.
LORD PAUL. Mind your own business.
IVY. What have you done?
LORD PAUL. I'm not supposed to have brought you here, or something.
MUTCH. We've made one new law today.
LORD PAUL. Well, make another.
MUTCH. We can't make a habit of it.
IVY. Lord Paul, assert yourself. Show them what you're made of.
LORD PAUL. Now, listen to me, Mutch . . .
MUTCH. No, I won't. They must go back at once.

   JACK *crosses to Mutch and takes him by the arm.*

JACK. Not on your life, old man. Just you lead me to Geraldine.
MUTCH. No.
LORD PAUL [*crossing to* R] It's best just to ignore them, Mr Amersham. Just walk straight past.

   LORD PAUL *exits* R.

MUTCH. You'll be extremely unpopular.

       LORD PAUL *re-enters* R.

LORD PAUL. Shut up!
JACK [*crossing to* R] Now, do what teacher says. Shut—as you might say—up.

      LORD PAUL *and* JACK *exit* R. MUTCH *follows them off.*

IVY [*taking Tom by the hand*] Come along. Don't be frightened.

      BINDWEED *threatens Ivy with the pitch-fork.*

Goodness, what a big toasting-fork you've got there.

      IVY *and* TOM *exit* R.
      BINDWEED *follows them off as—*
     the LIGHTS BLACK-OUT

      MUSIC *for Scene Change. Reprise of end of No.* 13.

SCENE 9

Exterior of Shop and Miss Catamole's Cottage.

Immediately following.

There is a small bench outside Miss Catamole's cottage. Outside the shop there is a bench above the barrel and stools L. *On the barrel there is a lantern and a tray with four glasses of cider.*

When the FRONT CLOTH *rises,* POTTER *is seated on the left end of the bench above the barrel and* GERALDINE *is seated on the right end.* MISS CATAMOLE *is on the stool* R *of the barrel and* ALBERT *is on the stool* L *of it. They are sitting lazily with their drinks and are softly singing, unaccompanied, " Let The Grass Grow". A lighthouse flashes distantly at regular intervals. After a few moments,* MUTCH, LORD PAUL, IVY, JACK, TOM *and* BINDWEED *enter up* R. LORD PAUL *moves down* R, *followed by* MUTCH. JACK *moves down* LC. IVY *stands* C. BINDWEED *and* TOM *stay up* R *on the rostrum.*

      The MUSIC *fades.*

MUTCH [*as they enter*] I warn you, sir, the people won't like it. The people won't like it.

     JACK *and* GERALDINE *come face to face.*
     There is a pause.

JACK [*finally*] Hullo.
GERALDINE. So you found me.
JACK. Did you think I wouldn't ?
GERALDINE. No. I suppose not.
IVY [*crossing to Geraldine; effusively*] Of course not. Oh, Miss Melford, what a wonderful idea of yours. The missing heiress. It'll make the front page again if it's handled properly.
GERALDINE [*rising; very excited*] Oh, that isn't why I did it. How dare you ? [*She crosses below Ivy to* L *of Jack*] We can't stay here. We must go at once. All three of us.
ALBERT [*rising and moving down* L] No! [*To Jack*] How did you get here ?
LORD PAUL. I think somehow it's my fault.
GERALDINE. It's all right. We're going at once. I'll get my things.

     GERALDINE *crosses to the exit down* L, *but is stopped by* ALBERT *who catches her hand.*

ALBERT. No. It isn't possible to go tonight. I don't know what'll come of it all, but don't worry so much, d—dear Geraldine.

     This arrests GERALDINE. JACK *is isolated* C.

JACK. Geraldine . .

     MOLLY *enters up* R, *sees Jack and crosses to him, walking on air.*

MOLLY. Oo-oooh! [*She stands and faces Jack. In ecstasy*] Never in all my wildest dreams!

SCENE 9   FREE AS AIR

The ISLAND GIRLS *enter up* R, *see Jack, gasp, cluster round him* [MUSIC]
and sit him on the bench RC.

GIRLS. Ooo-h!
A GIRL. Is he real? [*She touches Jack with one finger*] He *is*.
GIRLS. Ohhhhh!

The GIRLS *sink round Jack, gazing and chattering.*

MUTCH [*moving* C] Shut up, shut up, shut up!

The GIRLS *are silent.*

There'll be a revolution. Lord Paul, do you see what you've done? This is all your fault.

GREGORY *and the* ISLAND MEN *enter.*

LORD PAUL. Yes, I think perhaps it is.
GERALDINE [*crossing to* C] No, it's mine. I started it.

        "THE GIRL FROM LONDON"   No. 14

                ENSEMBLE

GERALDINE.   I'm the cause of all
                Outsiders aren't allowed
                One is one and rather fun
                But three's a crowd.

                I'm the girl from London
                I who ran away
                To a quiet island
                On a Summer's day.

ALBERT.   I'm the man who loved her
                And it seemed to me
                Uncles ought to marry
                To set their nephews free.

GIRLS.   See—where it all began.
                All this confusion
                 Began with a girl who ran
                To seek seclusion.

MISS CATAMOLE. I'm the maiden lady
                I who much deplored
                Unprovoked advances
                From a noble lord.

LORD PAUL.   I'm the wicked uncle
                This is what I did
                Blurted out in panic
                Where a lady hid.

CHORUS.   How—will the story end?
                In tears or laughter?
                The end will of course depend
                On what comes after.

IVY.	I'm the smart reporter Longing to report Coaxing wicked uncles To say more than they ought.
JACK.	I'm the dashing, flashing Hero in distress Lost a girl and found her Assisted by the Press.
CHORUS.	How—will the story end? In tears or laughter? The end will of course depend On what comes after.
MOLLY.	I'm the village maiden Born to peek and pine. Here's the man I dreamed of But he isn't mine. I'm the maiden Who loved the hero Who helped the reporter To coax the uncle Who pestered the lady Because of the nephew Who loved the girl from London She who ran away To a quiet island On a Summer's day On a Summer's day On a Summer's day.
CHORUS.	How will the story end? In tears or laughter? The end will of course depend On what comes after.
MOLLY. JACK. IVY. LORD PAUL. MISS CATAMOLE ALBERT. ALL.	I'm the maiden Who loved the hero Who helped the reporter To coax the uncle Who pestered the lady Because of the nephew Who loved the girl from London She who ran Who ran from the Press and the man And that's how the story all began But how will the story end? In tears or laughter? The end will of course depend On what comes after What comes after

CURTAIN

ACT II

SCENE 1

The terrace of the Big House. The following morning

The house with its entrance is L. *There is a balustrade across the back with steps* R *leading up to the rostrum. There is a table* C, *laid for breakfast for four. A long wicker chair is* L *of the table; two upright chairs stand above the table and one* R *of it. A small serving table stands up* C. *A speaking-tube links the wicker chair to the chair above the right end of the table.*

OPENING MUSIC   No. 15

When the CURTAIN *rises,* LORD PAUL *is seated in the wicker chair. He is wearing a dressing-gown in place of his jacket, which is over the back of his chair.* JACK *is seated* R *of the table, reading a copy of " The Geographical Magazine ".* ALBERT *is seated above the right end of the table. He wears a butler's apron. The music continues during the following business which is in dumb show.* JACK *has one elbow on the table.* LORD PAUL *picks up his cup, drinks, and replaces it. As he does so,* JACK *takes his elbow off the table, and the table rocks.* JACK *tears a page from his magazine and wedges it under the downstage right leg of the table.* LORD PAUL *rocks the table then takes a piece of toast and puts it under the front left leg.* JACK *and* LORD PAUL *look at each other.* ALBERT *drops the trick leg that makes the table steady. The other two look at him in awe.* IVY *enters from the house* L. *She is wearing beach pyjamas and sunglasses and carries a notebook and pencil.* LORD PAUL *rises a little,* ALBERT *completely,* JACK *not at all.* IVY *sits above the left end of the table.* ALBERT *indicates the side table up* C. IVY *rises.* LORD PAUL *half rises.* ALBERT *rises, goes to the side table and pours coffee for* IVY, *who sees his apron and happily makes a note of it. She is talking very fast but cannot be heard over the music.* IVY *takes her coffee and resumes her seat.* ALBERT *resumes his seat.* LORD PAUL *offers* IVY *an orange.* IVY *absentmindedly takes an orange and passes it to* ALBERT *who passes it to* JACK *who throws it to* LORD PAUL *who offers it to* IVY. *This game goes on until the music ceases, then* LORD PAUL *blows through the speaking tube.* ALBERT *listens at his end.*

LORD PAUL. More butter, please, Albert.

ALBERT *rises and exits to the house* L.

IVY [*ecstatically*] Oh, it's all so quaint. I could write a book about you, Lord Paul.
LORD PAUL [*preening*] Oh, could you?
IVY. I've never met any decayed gentry before. Oh, I don't mean that personally, of course: you're in your prime and every inch an aristocrat. Albert is, too, but he hasn't so many inches. Will you show me round after breakfast?
LORD PAUL. With the greatest of pleasure.
IVY. I could stay here the rest of my life. Couldn't you, Mr Amersham?
JACK. No.
IVY. Oh. I mean, of course, if there were mod. cons. and if it was only for a week or two.

ALBERT *enters from the house with a dish of butter which he puts on the table beside* IVY. *He then resumes his seat.*

Thank you. I was saying, Mr Postumous, I could stay here for the rest of my life.
ALBERT. I'm afraid you won't be allowed to.
LORD PAUL. Albert!
ALBERT. I'm sorry, Uncle. I know they're your guests, but they're also the thin end of the wedge.
IVY. Don't you think if we just stayed you'd get used to us?
ALBERT. No, never. The most we can do is to invite you both to the Coronation.
JACK }
IVY } *together; startled*] Coronation?
ALBERT. It's at sunset. The boat could take you back with the nine o'clock tide.
JACK [*incredulous*] Have you got a Queen?
ALBERT. Yes, we have now, thank you. [*He returns to his food*]

JACK *shrugs and returns to his magazine.* LORD PAUL *rises and removes his dressing-gown.* ALBERT *rises, moves to Lord Paul and helps him into his jacket.*

LORD PAUL. Well, shall we start our tour of inspection?
IVY [*rising*] Oh, yes, I'm ready pronto. Is there a map I could follow our route with?
LORD PAUL. Oh, no, there's never been a map.

IVY *crosses to* R, *playfully smacking Jack's face as she passes.* JACK *slaps Ivy's bottom.* ALBERT *moves up* C *and gets a tray from the side table.*

LORD PAUL *and* IVY *exit up* L.

ALBERT [*stacking the breakfast things on the tray*] Excuse me, Mr Amersham, how long has Geraldine been a friend of yours?
JACK [*shrugging*] Couple of years. She's been my girl friend for about six months.
ALBERT. Well, she's only been *my* girl friend for a day, but . . .
JACK. Not *girl* friend. Friend.
ALBERT. There's a difference?
JACK. Of course. A friend is someone you see occasionally. A girl friend is someone you're seen *with*.
ALBERT. Do girls like being seen with you?
JACK [*exasperated*] Mr Postumous! [*He rises and stands below the table*] If you've got your eye on Geraldine, you haven't got a hope.
ALBERT [*moving to* L *of Jack*] I've got lots of hopes.
JACK. No. She may have fallen for you and your island. That's natural—she's a woman. But it's me she'll come after in the end.
ALBERT. Why?
JACK [*shrugging*] Girls do. I'm a sort of magnet.

REPRISE

No. 16

"A MAN FROM THE MAINLAND"

MOLLY, JACK *and* GIRLS

MOLLY *is heard singing, unaccompanied off* R. JACK *and* ALBERT *speak over the singing.*

MOLLY [*off; singing*]
    Here am I imploring
    Nobody seems to hear
    I am keen to live and keen to learn
    I want a bath with a tap I can turn
    When will my man appear?

JACK [*over the singing*] Hear that? Sad, isn't it?
ALBERT. Sad?
JACK. It's me she wants.
ALBERT. Molly? Yes, she'd make a good wife.
JACK. Oh, she's charming, but I think I'll stick to Geraldine.

The MUSIC *ceases.*

MOLLY *and the* ISLAND GIRLS *enter up* R *and come down* RC.

ALBERT. You're very sure of yourself.
JACK. It's difficult for me not to be.

MOLLY *and the* GIRLS *cluster around Jack.*
ALBERT *watches for a while then exits into the house* L.
The MUSIC *recommences.*

SCENE 1 FREE AS AIR

MOLLY and GIRLS [*singing*]
We want a man from the mainland.
He has rent us half asunder,
And our souls would all be saleable
For a mainland kiss.
We *all* want a man from the mainland
We will swamp him 'til he's under
And we'll nail him if he's nailable
To an island miss.

Take us away.
Take us to London.
We're tied up in knots
And ready to be undone.
Hurry! Hurry! Oh!

JACK. They all want a man from the mainland
And I must say I don't wonder
When you think of what's available
In a place like this.
MOLLY *and the* GIRLS *cluster tightly round Jack.*

MOLLY and GIRLS. Take us away
Though we are shabby
It would be so gay
To marry in the Abbey
Hurry! Hurry! Oh!

We do want a man from the mainland
We are pining for him madly
To remove us to a sane land
And away from this inane land
For we're certain that the mainland
Is the place to be.

JACK *rushes off up* R.
MOLLY *and the* GIRLS *follow him off.*
GERALDINE *enters down* L, *looking for Jack.*
JACK *re-enters up* R *and creeps up to Geraldine.*

JACK. Geraldine! Geraldine, at last I've caught you. [*He holds her hands firmly*]
GERALDINE *tries to release herself.*
No, don't wriggle. [*Strongly*] Why did you run away?
GERALDINE [*strongly*] Why did you follow me?
JACK. Because I love you.
GERALDINE. You don't.
JACK [*releasing her*] I love you.
GERALDINE [*crossing to the exit* R] No.
JACK [*following Geraldine; plaintively*] If I didn't love you, why would I want to marry you?
GERALDINE [*stopping and turning; gently*] Once and for all, Jack . . .
JACK. Now, listen . . .
GERALDINE. It's absolutely final. I can't marry you. I'm not your sort.
JACK. But you could *change*, Geraldine. You could *adapt* yourself.
GERALDINE *laughs.*
Honestly, don't you think it's time I settled down?

GERALDINE. Yes. If you don't pretty soon, you never will.   MUSIC
JACK. Well, then . . . ?
GERALDINE. But not with me.
JACK. Geraldine . . .
GERALDINE. There's nothing more to be said. [*She moves very decisively to the exit* R, *but turns swiftly*] And another thing—if you love me, why did you let Ivy Crush come here ? Terhou's unsafe, now. I may have to leave here for ever.
JACK [*crossing to* LC] Of course you'll leave here for ever. [*He sits in Lord Paul's chair*]
GERALDINE. Oh! [*She turns impatiently to go*]

ALBERT *enters* L.

ALBERT. Geraldine! Geraldine, there's something I want to ask you. [*He looks at Jack*]

JACK *waves Albert across to Geraldine.*

GERALDINE. Yes ?
ALBERT [*crossing to Geraldine*] Will you be my g-girl friend ?
GERALDINE [*laughing*] Albert! Just for today ?
ALBERT. Oh, no. For a very long time. I love you.
GERALDINE. Love me ?
JACK. Do carry on as if I wasn't here.
ALBERT. Thank you.
JACK. Not at all.
ALBERT. Do you love me at all ?
GERALDINE. Don't ask me now, Albert. I may have to go away.
ALBERT [*appalled*] Go away ?
JACK. *Of course* you'll go away.
GERALDINE. If Ivy won't keep quiet about Terhou . . .
JACK. She won't.
GERALDINE. We'll make her.
JACK. She won't.
GERALDINE. Then I shall *have* to go. Or they'll be down like a pack of wolves with television cameras.
JACK. Have you ever seen a wolf with a television camera ?
ALBERT. *I've* never seen a wolf.
JACK [*rising and crossing to Geraldine*] What *is* all this nonsense about staying here ? Do you think you can manage without London ?
GERALDINE. I managed for years. You forget I'm a country girl.
JACK [*glaring at Albert*] Something's gone to your head—and if you ask me it isn't the island.
GERALDINE. Jack!
JACK. Don't you "Jack" me. I'm going to find Molly.

JACK *exits up* R.

GERALDINE [*laughing gaily*] Poor Jack. He likes to be with people who appreciate him.
ALBERT. Geraldine! Don't laugh. You said you might have to go away.
GERALDINE. Only "might".
ALBERT. For ever ?

ALBERT *and* GERALDINE *move down* C.

GERALDINE. Only "might", Albert. Don't worry yet, it's early in the day.

The FRONT CLOTH *falls behind Albert and Geraldine.*

"I'D LIKE TO BE LIKE YOU"

No. 17

ALBERT and GERALDINE

SCENE 2

The Gorse Front Cloth

GERALDINE [*speaking over the music*] You look so unhappy.
ALBERT. I'm ashamed of myself for being so stupid. I had no idea—no idea that the Press could be so . . . Ivy Crush is just a *nice, silly* girl.
GERALDINE. Yes.
ALBERT. I don't understand anything. I'm a barbarian.
GERALDINE. You, of all people!
ALBERT. I wish I were like you and knew the world.
GERALDINE. What good has it done me?
ALBERT. What good? You're wise—and brave—and clever—and understanding—and wise—and brave—
GERALDINE. Albert! Stop.
ALBERT. —and beautiful.
GERALDINE. Listen, dear Albert, I could say *you* were all those things, too.
ALBERT. Even beautiful? Honestly, I wish I were like you. How long would it take me to learn your way of life?
GERALDINE. I'd rather learn yours.
ALBERT. Mine? There's nothing to learn.
GERALDINE. Oh, but there is. [*She sings*]
Your world is so inviting, would it receive me?
ALBERT. Your world is so exciting, won't you believe me?
BOTH. I'd spend my days
Learning your ways
Earning your praise.

GERALDINE. I'd like to be like you
So free and bright and new
I'd like to be much less like me
And more like you.

ALBERT. Oh, how I'd like to be
So bright and new and free
And think and do much more like you
And less like me.

BOTH. Instruct me, teach me, show me
It takes no time to know me.
But I must make a start, if I'm
To learn each part of you by heart.

If here upon this beach
We settled down to teach
Would we be loth to be like both
And less like each?

ALBERT. I'd like to be like you
And share your point of view
So much, you see, is strange to me
And clear to you.

GERALDINE.	Oh, how I'd like to be High up where I could see The kind of view that's clear to you And strange to me
BOTH.	Oh, start my education Oh, share your information. You've quite enough for two. Oh, tell me How you grew to be like you. We mustn't make a fuss We'll argue and discuss Until we're unlike either one And more like us.

MUSIC

GERALDINE *and* ALBERT *exit as—*

the LIGHTS BLACK-OUT

SCENE 3

The Well. Later the same morning.

A ladder-back chair is set R *with Miss Catamole's knitting on it. There is a basket of seaweed* L.
When the FRONT CLOTH *rises several pieces of seaweed are decoratively hung on the well.* MISS CATAMOLE *is standing on the well, putting the finishing touches.* POTTER *is assisting her.*

MISS CATAMOLE [*after a moment*] Have you got a bit more of the pink, Mr Potter?

POTTER *hands Miss Catamole a piece of seaweed.*

Thank you. [*She hangs the seaweed on the well*]
POTTER. It's in good condition. Not too wet and not too dry.
MISS CATAMOLE. Do you think a touch more green?
POTTER. I'm uncertain, Miss Catamole.
MISS CATAMOLE. Would you mind taking the long view?
POTTER [*stepping back*] The short pink piece should go a little to the left.

MISS CATAMOLE *moves the seaweed.*

Stop! That's it. Now, if you were to substitute the piece you're wearing . . .

MISS CATAMOLE *takes a piece of seaweed from round her neck and drapes it on the well.*

Yes. The balance is perfect. Excuse me. [*He suddenly darts forward and selects a piece of seaweed from the base of the well*] I thought so. I'm afraid you can't have this. Only second and third standard for the decorations. First standard for the mainland trade.
MISS CATAMOLE. Is that a bit of the choice?
POTTER. Yes. It can't be spared. It's been a goodish crop but it's not a vintage year.
MISS CATAMOLE [*coming down and moving* R] It *does* look nice.
POTTER. You have an eye for colour, Miss Catamole.
MISS CATAMOLE [*pleased*] Really? Oh, can't you see Miss Melford sitting there? Won't she be the most beautiful Queen we ever had?
POTTER. No, Miss Catamole.

MISS CATAMOLE *looks at Potter.*

You were the most beautiful Queen we ever had. [*He does not appear to know he has said it*] I'll just put this back. [*He puts the surplus seaweed into the basket* L]

MISS CATAMOLE *picks up her knitting, sits in the chair* R *and knits.*

SCENE 8   FREE AS AIR

                    LORD PAUL *enters busily up* L, *carrying an armful of books.*   MUSIC
                    IVY *follows him on. She carries a tape recorder, her camera and
                    a notebook and pencil. She puts the recorder and camera on the
                    ground up* R.

LORD PAUL [*as he enters*]   Well, the well is the political centre of the island and would be a good spot to base our operations. [*Generally*] Miss Crush is interested in our folk songs and traditions.
IVY [*to Miss Catamole*]   Oh, very interested.
MISS CATAMOLE.   How very interesting.
IVY [*crossing to Miss Catamole*] Can you tell me anything about the folk songs and traditions, Miss Catamole ?
MISS CATAMOLE [*cheerfully*]   No.
IVY.   Oh, come ! There must be *something*.
MISS CATAMOLE [*interested*]   Really ?
IVY [*crossing to Potter*]   Mr Potter—they tell me you go gathering seaweed, Mr Potter. Do tell me what it's made into.
                    LORD PAUL *sits on the well.*
POTTER.   Now, I *did* know.
IVY.   Lord Paul ?
LORD PAUL [*turning the pages of a book; knowledgeably*] Yes—er . . .
MISS CATAMOLE.   *Young* Mr Postumous will know.
                    LORD PAUL *reacts.*
POTTER [*reminded*]   Albert ! Yes, it's used to make soundproof walls.
IVY.   Well ! Would you believe it !
POTTER.   No.   You'd think it'd come cheaper not to make a noise.
                    POTTER *picks up the basket of seaweed and exits with it over the
                    wall up* L.
MISS CATAMOLE.   Of course it's used for other things, too. Medicine and glue, for instance.
LORD PAUL.   Really, Miss Catamole, there's no end. It's all here in the book. Under " Trades ", you see—though it doesn't seem to mention soundproof walls. [*He blows between the pages and a cloud of dust rises*] And here—" History—The Islands have many interesting remains ". Miss Crush—at this very moment I am sitting patiently on a monument. This stone. It has an inscription : I'll unveil it. [*He rises*]
                    IVY *moves down* L *of the well.*
IVY [*reading*]   " Testudo semper libera."
                    LORD PAUL *sits on the well.*   IVY *sits* L *of Lord Paul on the well.*
LORD PAUL.   " Testudo " is, of course, the Latin for turtle, and the obvious derivation of the island's present name—Terhou.
IVY [*trying to see the connection*]   Er–obvious ?
LORD PAUL.   Yes. It's perfectly simple.
                    POTTER *enters over the wall up* L, *carrying a long piece of seaweed.
                    He sits on the wall.*
The Romans called the island Testudo because it looked like a turtle rising out of the sea. Then came the pirates from the north. They referred to the island as Hou.
IVY.   Why ?
LORD PAUL.   Hou is, of course, the Norse for island.
IVY [*making notes in shorthand*]   Fancy !
LORD PAUL.   By a gradual process of corruption—which I won't go into—turtle and hou became amalgamated to form the name Terhou.
IVY [*writing*]   Ter-hou.   Yes ?
LORD PAUL.   That's all.
IVY.   Ter-hou.   Ter—   Oh !   Terhou !   Terhou !
   D

LORD PAUL. Jug-jug.   MUSIC
IVY. We've got there. Thank you, Lord Paul.
LORD PAUL. The island was occupied by the Romans and liberated in fifty-four B.C. by Queen Gulfrog, who was forced to buy its freedom by sacrificing her innocence.
IVY. How exciting!
LORD PAUL. The Roman chief was called Sextus Postumous Lascivius.
IVY. Your ancestor.
LORD PAUL. Gulfrog begged him to leave. He agreed to do so if she went with him. And Gulfrog complied.
IVY. How brave.
LORD PAUL. He is said to have been a very handsome man. Some years later she returned here to Testudo bringing a son with her.
MISS CATAMOLE. That reminds me of something—there *was* a song.
IVY. A folk song?
MISS CATAMOLE. Telling that story about Testudo. [*She sings*] Testudo, Testudo . . . [*She breaks off*] But I can't remember the words.
LORD PAUL. I've remembered *my* part.
IVY [*eagerly*] Yes?
LORD PAUL. Yes. [*He sings, mainly on one note*] La, la, la, la, la . . . It's the bass part, of course.
IVY [*flatly*] Yes.
POTTER [*without warning; singing his harmony*] La, la, la, la, la!

> MISS CATAMOLE *rises, puts down her knitting and moves to* R *of Lord Paul.*

MISS CATAMOLE. The tenor! Let's do them together.

> LORD PAUL *rises and puts the book on the well.* POTTER *rises and moves to* L *of Lord Paul.* IVY *rises, collects her tape recorder, takes it down* L *and opens it.*

Lord Paul, you come underneath.

> MISS CATAMOLE, LORD PAUL *and* POTTER *sing a phrase in harmony.*

IVY. Splendid! Now, all we want are the words and the tune.
MISS CATAMOLE. Mr Mutch will know.
IVY [*calling*] Mr Mutch.
ALL [*calling*] Mr Mutch.

> MUTCH, *unseen by* LORD PAUL, *enters up* L.

LORD PAUL [*calling through his megaphone*] Mutch!

> MUTCH *moves down* LC.

Oh, there you are. You remember a song about Testudo?
MUTCH [*promptly singing*] " Oh, island, my island, Testudo . . ."
IVY. Oh, wait. My recorder. [*She sets out the microphone*]   Ready now.

> MOLLY, BINDWEED, GREGORY, TOM *and the* ISLAND GIRLS *and* MEN *enter.* MOLLY *and* BINDWEED *move down* L. POTTER, LORD PAUL *and* MISS CATAMOLE *form a group* R *with the rest of the* ISLANDERS. MUTCH *fussily organizes everyone, then blows the chord on his pitch pipe.* IVY *switches on the tape recorder.*

" TESTUDO "   No. 18

ENSEMBLE

MUTCH.   Oh, island, my island, Testudo, Testudo,
            You knelt to fair Gulfrog and bitterly cried:
CHORUS.   " These Romans so crude-o intrude-o Testudo,
            They eat all our food-o since we're occupied."

SCENE 8 — FREE AS AIR

MUTCH. Said you:
CHORUS. "See our grief-o,
Would Gulfrog be lief-o,
To speak with their chief-o?"
And Gulfrog complied.

MOLLY. "Postumous Lascivius, you come here to chivvy us,
It's rude-o Testudo, and bad for our pride."

LORD PAUL commences the chorus too soon and is stopped by MISS CATAMOLE.

CHORUS. The lord of the island—Testudinis, Testudinis,
Took rough hold of Gulfrog but softly replied:
BINDWEED. "I'll straight leave the island, Testudinem, Testudinem,
If you will come too, as my unlawful bride."

CHORUS. Said she: "You are thieves-o,
But how my breast heaves-o."
He threw off his greaves-o
And Gulfrog complied.
So she was their saviour through her loose behaviour,
A prude—o Testudo, would rather have died.

ALL. So drink to the island, Testudini, Testudini,
Where white blow the breakers and high runs the tide.
Remember when nude-o, with woad you were blued-o,
With Romans so lewd-o, you were occupied.
A maid was subdued-o
And now you include-o
A lord of Testudo
Whom Gulfrog supplied.
I wot that her capture was not without rapture,
Conclude-o Testudo where high runs the tide.

JACK enters up L and crosses on the rostrum to R. IVY switches off the recorder and collects the microphone.

ALL exit except MOLLY who moves up R. JACK catches her hand as she passes.

MOLLY. Why did you do that?
JACK. How about showing me the island?
MOLLY. I've got to go fishing.
JACK. Well, we'll go fishing together.
MOLLY. I expect you've caught some pretty big fish in your time.
JACK. Well—er . . .
MOLLY. I expect you're good at almost everything.

JACK expertly takes Molly in his arms and kisses her.

Oh, yes. You are.
JACK. You're not so bad yourself.
MOLLY. Oh, I've been practising. [*She crosses to the well and sits*]
JACK. Have you? [*He sits beside Molly on the well*]
MOLLY. I wanted to impress you.
JACK. Keep trying. You know, you're the sort of girl I've been looking for.
MOLLY [*ecstatically*] This is something that is going to last for ever.
JACK. You haven't mentioned me to your mother?
MOLLY [*leaping into Jack's lap*] I haven't got a mother, or anybody except you.
JACK. Steady on. old girl.

MOLLY. Mr Amersham, do you love me?
JACK. Well, now ...
MOLLY [*rising and crossing down* R] You don't. You love Miss Melford.
JACK [*rising and moving down* C] I don't. She's turned me down.
MOLLY. Oh, then you're free. [*She rushes at Jack and flings her arms around him*] When do we start?
JACK. Start? Start what?
MOLLY. For London.
JACK. Any time you like.
MOLLY. Oh, Jack.
JACK. You don't know what you're taking on.
MOLLY. I do. I know all about London. Lord Paul showed me some photographs once. I'm going to ride in horseless carriages and drink coffee, gallons of it.
JACK. So you really want to leave the island?
MOLLY. Yes. I'm in a beautiful dream.
JACK [*moving to the well and sitting*] Oh, dear!

"I'VE GOT MY FEET ON THE GROUND" No. 19

JACK AND MOLLY

MOLLY *sits beside Jack on the well. Throughout this number, until the last phrase,* JACK *sings with firmness, whilst* MOLLY *sings amorously. The last phrase is mutually romantic.*

MOLLY [*speaking over the music*] Oh, Jack, don't you ever dream?
JACK. No, I gave it up years ago. [*He sings*]

> Don't be too hasty, darling.
> I love you, you know that,
> But don't let's be carried away
> Or do anything to which we might say "Drat!"

MOLLY
> I want to be hasty, darling,
> For frankly I can't wait.
> I want to be carried away,
> To Notting Hill Arch and Marble Gate.

JACK.
> I'm using common sense,
> I'm not jumping fences.

MOLLY.
> My common sense
> Is driven away
> By some very uncommon senses.

JACK.
> I've got my feet on the ground.
MOLLY.
> I've got my head in the clouds.
> I hope I never know too much about you.
JACK.
> I've got my feet on the ground.
MOLLY.
> I've got my head in the clouds.
> I hope you never give me cause to doubt you.

JACK.
> I wouldn't bank too much
> Or swank too much about me.
> Maybe after a week of me
> You'll shriek at me and clout me.

SCENE 8   FREE AS AIR

MOLLY.   I've got my feet on the ground.
            I've got my head in the clouds.
            I hope that I can stay
            This way for ever,
BOTH.   Stay this way at least
            Until the end of to –
MOLLY [*speaking over the music*] Oh, Jack! I'd like to be the only woman in your life, but if not, could I be one of the crowd?
JACK.   You'd be very noticeable.
MOLLY. When we get to London, what's the first thing I shall see?
JACK.   A long line of factories, from London Airport to Waterloo.
MOLLY. Where shall we live? In Mayfair?
JACK.   Number five twenty-three, Cromwell Road.
MOLLY. Oh! Everything about you is so romantic.
JACK [*singing*] I think you've yearned enough
            And churned enough
            For one day.
            You may find an inspired romance
            A tired romance by Monday.

            I've got my feet on the ground.
MOLLY.   I've got my head in the clouds
            I hope that I can stay
            This way for ever,
BOTH.   Stay this way at least
            Until the end of today.

                        JACK *and* MOLLY *embrace. Cheering is heard off* R.
                        MOLLY *and* JACK *rise and rush off up* L.
                        BINDWEED *enters down* R.
                        GREGORY *enters down* L.

BINDWEED [*after a moment*] Mr Gregory.
GREGORY. Yes, Mr Bindweed?
BINDWEED. Are you aware of what's going on?
GREGORY. Sometimes, Mr Bindweed.
BINDWEED. I mean now.

                        The cheering increases.

Hear that?
GREGORY. Whatever is it?
BINDWEED. It's that *other* woman. She's exciting the mob. " Ivy " they call her, and she's poisonous all right. Creeps over everything. Would you believe it, when she sees my campion meadow—" Oh, my! " she says. " That'll make a nice caravan site." " There'll by no camping on my campions," says I. " They're champion campions, all of 'em, and don't you dare touch a hair of their heads."
GREGORY. That finished her, I bet.
BINDWEED. Not her. She's everlasting, that one.
GREGORY. I wonder if she's staying long.
BINDWEED. Oh, she's bedded in all right. Her roots are beginning to show already. So be on your guard, Mr Gregory.

                    " HOLIDAY ISLAND " (PART I)   No. 20
                                ENSEMBLE

                        During the introduction IVY, LORD PAUL, MUTCH, POTTER *and*
                        MISS CATAMOLE *enter down* R.

The ISLAND MEN *and* GIRLS *with* TOM *and* MOLLY *enter in twos and threes.* IVY *crosses to* C. [MUSIC]

IVY [*singing*]. Do you want to be popular?
ALL. Yes, we want to be popular.
IVY. Do you want to be famous?
ALL. Yes, we want to be famous.

IVY. You can be both if you listen to me,
I know what your island ought to be.

ALL. What ought we to be? What ought we to be?
There's nobody as innocent and ignorant as we.
Tell us what we ought to be.

IVY. The perfect place for a family vacation,
The tourist's dream of retarded civilization.
No-one here since the Roman occupation,
With all the old original sanitation.
Primitive! Barbaric!
A home from home!
In fact a holiday
On the Continent,
British at the same time
Come without a passport.
Here's our Holiday Island.

GERALDINE, JACK *and* ALBERT *enter up* R.

ALL. Thank you for telling us.
Now that we know,
We'll make our island the place to go
For a happy holiday.

GERALDINE, JACK *and* ALBERT.
What an idiotic thing to say
On a happy holiday island
You would all be very unhappy
They would never let you alone,
You would never have a moment of your own.

On a jolly holiday island
You would soon be very unjolly.
They would not allow you to yawn,
You would wakey-wakey-wakey with the dawn.

Just imagine it! Just imagine it!
Think of being charming to the trippers.
Just imagine it! Just imagine it!
Think of all the oranges and kippers.

If you once converted the island,
To a joyful holiday island,
Any chance of joy would be small,
For you'd never have a holiday at all.

There'd be gran'mas hauling brollies around;
There'd be urchins mauling lollies around;
There'd be ice cream queues,
And the football news,
And a ruddy great gramophone playing the blues.

> There'd be landed gentry landed on you,
> There'd be flossy candy candied on you,
> There'd be knobbly knees
> And a smell of cheese.

MUSIC

The MUSIC *stops suddenly.*

JACK. Well, here we are on Terhou—so called because when the Romans landed they said, " It's too good to be terhou." Pardon my Latin ! Now, here on Holiday Island your pleasure is our business. And to make sure you enjoy every marvellous minute of it, let's start by breathing in the wonderful ozone. Just try breathing, you'll love it. [*He pulls Lord Paul to* c] Come on, Dad. Show 'em how to do it. In, out, in, out, in—breathing, breathing, breathing. It tones up your posture, puts roses in your cheeks, gives you an appetite. In fact, it puts life into you.

LORD PAUL *collapses.* MISS CATAMOLE *helps him to stand up.*

Ah, that's right. Getting together. Getting to know you. Getting to know all about you. You come here a bachelor, you'll take home a wife. You come here with a wife, you'll take home two. And do you know why ? Because you're never allowed to be lonely. Not for a single minute, and to make sure you're not we've got a grand comedy swimming gala. Don't forget your water-wings. We've got a " Duck-your-best-friend " competition. Don't forget your best friend ; and we've got a *long cross country* run. So keep smiling. Keep going. And remember, if we can't all be beautiful you can be healthy.

" HOLIDAY ISLAND " (PART II)

No. 20a

ENSEMBLE

JACK [*singing*]
> Oh gosh, it will be fun
> To be blistered by the sun.
> There's a sun-tan competition
> Simply waiting to be won.
> Breakfast is at six ;
> It's compulsory to mix,
> Remember we're a family
> A jolly bunch of bricks.
> We'll be hiking,
> We'll be biking,
> No matter what the weather,
> And everything we do
> We will do together.
> Don't give in to indigestion,
> Answer me this simple question
> Are we going to make the party go ?
> Are we happy ?

ALL.
> No ! No ! No !

> On a happy holiday island,
> We would all be very unhappy,
> We would have to cover the tracks
> Of plutocrats escaping from the tax.
> If we once converted the island
> To a joyful holiday island,
> Any chance of joy would be small,
> For we'd never have a holiday,
> We'd never have a holiday,
> We'd never have a holiday at all.

>   BINDWEED, GREGORY, MOLLY *and the* ISLAND GIRLS *and* MEN MUSIC
>   *exit.* LORD PAUL *sits on the chair* R. JACK, GERALDINE *and*
>   ALBERT *cluster around Lord Paul.* MUTCH *and* POTTER *sit on the*
>   *well.* IVY *stands down* L. MISS CATAMOLE *and* TOM *stand* LC.

GERALDINE. Now, do you understand, Lord Paul, why it would be fatal to let Ivy exploit you?
JACK. You're nursing a viper in your bosom.

> LORD PAUL *springs up in alarm.*

ALBERT. Obviously, Uncle, we must keep Miss Crush from talking.
JACK. However difficult that may be.
ALBERT. She mustn't get in touch with the Press. We must keep her on the island.
GERALDINE. Yes. She's dangerous.
JACK. She's dynamite! [*He moves and sits on the rostrum up* R]
MUTCH. She must be locked up.

> *There is a pause. They all look at Ivy.*

LORD PAUL [*crossing to* C] Very well. [*To Ivy. Regretfully*] I'm extremely sorry.
IVY. Oh, I'm used to being treated rough. [*She smiles at Lord Paul and crosses to* L *of him*]
LORD PAUL [*pulling himself together*] Mutch! Do your duty!

> MUTCH *rises and moves to* L *of Ivy.*

MUTCH. I arrest you in the name of Terhou.
IVY [*holding out her hands to be handcuffed*] What fun! I'm quite ready, Officer.
MUTCH. Where to, Lord Paul?
LORD PAUL. Oh—er—gaol, I suppose.
MUTCH. We haven't got a gaol.
LORD PAUL. What? [*To Potter*] Bailiff! What have you done with the gaol?
POTTER [*rising and moving down* L] You gave orders for it to be turned into a dairy.
LORD PAUL. Oh, did I? Well, turn it back again.
POTTER. That's impossible.
MUTCH. Then we shall have to use the stocks.
IVY. Oh, how quaint: You're almost mediaeval.
LORD PAUL [*sternly*] Potter! Stocks!
POTTER. Oh, yes. [*He moves towards his house* L]
LORD PAUL. Where are they?
POTTER [*stopping and turning*] I'm using them as a fender.
LORD PAUL. Bring them forth.
POTTER. Yes, Lord Paul.

> POTTER *exits to the house* L.
> TOM *follows him off.*

LORD PAUL. Sorry to keep you waiting, Miss Crush.
MUTCH. Have you ever done time before?

> POTTER *and* TOM *enter from the house* L *carrying the stocks and some cushions.*

IVY. Not since . . . [*She sees the stocks. Enraptured*] Oh, aren't they historic!
ALBERT. You like them?
LORD PAUL. Several people have died in them.
IVY. I can't wait to try them on.
MUTCH. Just try them for size, Miss Crush.

> POTTER *places the stocks in front of the well.* TOM *sets the cushions.*
> IVY *sits in the stocks and puts one foot in place.* POTTER *is* L *of*
> *her,* LORD PAUL R *of her.*

LORD PAUL. Now, put the other one in.

> IVY *puts her other foot in place.*

POTTER. They're a beautiful fit.
IVY. Now! Shut me up!
MISS CATAMOLE. That was the intention.

       LORD PAUL *closes and locks the stocks.*

MUTCH. Tt, tt! Your shoes are very muddy. [*He polishes Ivy's shoes*]
LORD PAUL. Is there anything you'd like?
MISS CATAMOLE. Another cushion?
MUTCH. A cup of tea?
POTTER. A glass of beer?
ALBERT. A *Geographical Magazine*?
MUTCH. Lord Paul, how long is the term of imprisonment to be?
LORD PAUL. Why—er—until Miss Crush undertakes to keep quiet about Terhou.
JACK. No scoop, Ivy.
IVY. Oh, but it's already on its way.

         JACK *rises.*

GERALDINE. What?
IVY. The scoop. They ought to be here by this afternoon.
ALBERT [*threateningly*] Who are *they*?
IVY. Oh, they'll be the very *pick* of the *Daily Echo*.

      Sensation. GERALDINE *crosses to Ivy.*

GERALDINE. You sent a message to the mainland, after all?
IVY. You wouldn't want me to lose my job, would you?
GERALDINE. How did you send it?
IVY [*losing confidence*] By telegram. The dear little ferryman took it.
LORD PAUL. Tom, come here.

       TOM *crosses to Lord Paul.*

Did you send a telegram?
TOM. Yes, Lord Paul. She said it was for her ailing mother. [*He takes a crumpled piece of paper from his pocket and hands it to Lord Paul*]
MISS CATAMOLE. Tom can't read, you know.
LORD PAUL [*reading*] " Daily Echo, one hundred and forty-six Fleet Street, London, E.C. Geraldine Melford located on Terhou twenty miles west Jersey stop possible scoop of the year stop send reinforcements immediately stop Ivy Crush stop stop Melford Crush Crush."
GERALDINE. I must go! I must go!
ALBERT. Geraldine!
GERALDINE. I must. I'm the cause of this. I'm the only one who can stop it.
ALBERT. Let me come with you.
GERALDINE. No! And keep her there. Let her send no more messages.

        REPRISE

      " HOLIDAY ISLAND "

       CHANGE OF SCENE

      GERALDINE *runs across the rostrum and exits up* L. *The others all follow her, leaving* IVY *alone as—*

    the FRONT CLOTH *falls*

SCENE 4

The Shore Front Cloth. The afternoon of the same day

GERALDINE *enters* L. *She is wearing a mackintosh.* ALBERT *follows her on.*

The MUSIC *fades.*

GERALDINE. Please, don't follow me, Albert. I'll just collect my things and go.
ALBERT. You can't go.
GERALDINE [*rapidly*] There's no other way. If they find me here, Terhou will be a front-page story. You know what that means. I'll meet them in Jersey and tell them—something.
ALBERT. Geraldine . . .
GERALDINE. I ought never to have come here. I'll forget I ever came and so must you.
ALBERT. But you'll come back?
GERALDINE. No.
ALBERT. When this is over?
GERALDINE. It would only happen again. Don't you see, I'm news.
ALBERT. There must be some other way.
GERALDINE. There isn't.
ALBERT. I'll think of something—only give me time.
GERALDINE. It's too late.
ALBERT. You can't go now. There's a heavy mist.
GERALDINE. Good. That'll delay them. [*She takes a letter from her pocket and hands it to Albert*] This letter's for you. Don't open it till after I've gone. [*She cannot look at him*] Good-bye, Albert. No, don't come and see me off. *Please.* Let me go alone.
ALBERT. I wanted to tell you I—I—I . . .
GERALDINE. I know. There isn't time.

GERALDINE *runs off* R. *After a moment,* ALBERT *turns and exits* L, *opening Geraldine's letter as he goes.*

SCENE 5

The Seashore. Later that afternoon.

When the FRONT CLOTH *rises,* POTTER *is sitting on the upturned boat, gazing out to sea.* TOM *enters up* R, *carrying Geraldine's luggage.* GERALDINE *follows him on. She is arrested at the sight of Potter.* TOM *climbs over the wall up* L.

GERALDINE. How long, Tom?
TOM [*shrugging*] A few minutes.

TOM *disappears over the wall.*

GERALDINE [*crossing to Potter*] Mr Potter.
POTTER. Oh. Hullo, Miss Melford. It's misty for going over.
GERALDINE. Do you think I shall get there?
POTTER [*reassuringly*] Oh, yes, you'll get there.
GERALDINE [*sitting beside Potter on the boat*] There's something you could do for me before I go.
POTTER. Certainly.
GERALDINE. Something went wrong yesterday and it was my fault. You could help me to put it right.
POTTER. Yes?
GERALDINE. You're fond of Miss Catamole, aren't you?
POTTER [*heartily*] Yes. Very.
GERALDINE. Why don't you ask her to marry you?
POTTER. Oh, I did.
GERALDINE [*very surprised*] She refused you?
POTTER. Oh, no.

SCENE 5] FREE AS AIR

MUSIC

GERALDINE. What then?
POTTER. Well, I didn't exactly *ask* her. I went *intending* to ask her, and then [*trying to remember*] she was—out . . .
GERALDINE. And you didn't try again?
POTTER. Oh, I *shall*, of *course*. [*With smiling embarrassment*] A man has to screw himself up.
GERALDINE. Well, you must. How long is it since the first try?
POTTER [*after thinking*] Fifteen years.

GERALDINE *becomes suddenly active, rises, pulls* POTTER *to his feet and pushes him* C.

GERALDINE. Now, tidy yourself. I mean, shake the dust off a bit. [*She pats his coat*] And square your shoulders. And put your hat at the right angle. [*She adjusts his hat*] And pick a bunch of flowers.
POTTER. The flowers are all picked for the Coronation.
GERALDINE. You'll find some. Carry a bunch in your left hand. Say, " I've brought you these flowers, Miss Catamole," and then, " Will you marry me? "
POTTER. Would that be enough?
GERALDINE. Quite enough. Now practise. Pretend I'm Miss Catamole. You're coming to see me. [*She sits on the boat*]
POTTER. Yes.
GERALDINE. Come on.

POTTER *mimes.*

What are you doing?
POTTER. Knocking at the door.
GERALDINE. Oh, yes. Come in.

POTTER *mimes opening the door and entering.*

POTTER. I've brought you these flowers, Miss Catamole.
GERALDINE. Oh, thank you very much, Mr Potter.

There is a pause.

Go on.
POTTER. I didn't know she'd say anything.
GERALDINE. It doesn't matter if she does. Go on.
POTTER. Will you marry me?
GERALDINE. Thank you, Mr Potter. I would be very happy. [*She rises*] Now, go along.
POTTER. Now?
GERALDINE. Of course.
POTTER. Oh, I didn't know you meant now.
GERALDINE. When else? Go *along*, Mr Potter. She's fond of you.
POTTER. Really?
GERALDINE. Yes, I know she is. I happen to know.
POTTER. Oh, all right, then. [*He goes up* R *then stops and turns*]
GERALDINE [*prompting*] I've brought you these flowers.
POTTER. Oh, yes. [*He prompts himself as he goes*] Will you marry me? Will you marry me? Will you marry me?

GERALDINE'S EXIT No. 21

POTTER *exits up* R. TOM *appears over the wall up* L *and stands waiting.* GERALDINE *looks around, then goes to* TOM *as—*

the FRONT CLOTH *falls*

Scene 6

The Shore Front Cloth. Later that afternoon

JACK *enters* L. ALBERT *follows him on.*

The MUSIC *fades.*

ALBERT [*calling*] Mr Amersham.

JACK *stops* C *and turns.*

[*He crosses to Jack*] Mr Amersham, can I have a word with you?
JACK. I say, I wish you'd call me "Jack".
ALBERT. But you're leaving today.
JACK [*plaintively*] You can call me "Jack" for a couple of hours, can't you?
ALBERT. Oh yes. Would you care to call me "Albert"?
JACK. Delighted.

They shake hands.

ALBERT. There's something you can do for me, if you will.
JACK. Pleasure, old man.
ALBERT. It's this: Geraldine gave me a letter to open after she'd gone.
JACK. Very dramatic.
ALBERT. Yes. And she's given us her money.
JACK. All of it?
ALBERT. Nearly all of it. [*He takes the letter from his pocket*]
JACK. To you?
ALBERT. To the island, of course. [*He takes a cheque from the envelope and hands it to Jack*] Uncle Paul has the Terhou account in a Jersey bank.
JACK [*gazing at the cheque*] Well!
ALBERT [*reading Geraldine's letter*] She says, "I want Terhou to have the money. But on no account let the Press know." That's underlined. "I wish . . ." Oh, the rest's a bit private, if you'll excuse me.
JACK [*returning the cheque to Albert*] Well! Get her!
ALBERT [*busily*] That's what I intend to do. I've got an idea for saving her. You see, Geraldine left the island to save the island, like Gulfrog.
JACK. Like what?
ALBERT. Gulfrog. In fifty-four B.C. Postumous Lascivius . . .
JACK. Yes, never mind that now. Tell me your idea.
ALBERT. It's rather good, but I'll need your help because for the first time in my life I'm going to the mainland. I shall use Uncle Paul's boat.
JACK. And you want to know how to cross roads and so on.
ALBERT. Yes. Now this is my idea . . .

HURRY MUSIC   No. 21a

JACK *and* ALBERT *exit* R *as—*

the LIGHTS BLACK-OUT

Scene 7

The Bar of the Octopus Hotel. Early evening of the same day.

"GERALDINE"   No. 22

REPORTERS

When the FRONT CLOTH *rises,* FRANÇOIS *is behind the bar. The three* REPORTERS *are down* C, *with Ivy's telegram.*

1ST REPORTER.   Geraldine Melford located on Terhou

1st and 2nd Reporters.	Geraldine Melford located on Terhou.
	Where or what or who is "Terhou"?
	Haven't got a clue, not a clue.
Trio.	Geraldine Melford located on Terhou,
	Geraldine Melford located on Terhou,
	Geraldine Melford located on Terhou,
	Geraldine located
	She will be repatriated
	When we find that bally-hi or bally-hoo
	We refer to as " Terhou-di-ood-ly-ooh."

The Music *stops. The* Reporters *" discover " the bar and go up to it.* Geraldine *enters up* L *and sits on the chair down* L, *facing front.*

1st Reporter [*to François*] Three large Scotch.
François. Oui, monsieur. [*He pours three drinks*]
2nd Reporter. When's the next boat to Terhou?
François. I couldn't say, monsieur.
3rd Reporter [*turning to Geraldine*] Do you happen to know, miss?
Geraldine [*turning*] No.
Reporters [*together*] Geraldine! We've looked everywhere for you.
Geraldine [*to François*] I've been here all the time, haven't I?
François. Sans doute, madame.

The Reporters *cluster round Geraldine in a close group.*

1st Reporter. Ivy Crush told us you were at a place called Terhou.
Geraldine. There's no such place. I invented it to get rid of Ivy.
3rd Reporter. Aah! Trying to escape us again. You had us worried this time.
Geraldine. I'm sure I did.
1st Reporter. You mean a lot to us, Geraldine.
2nd Reporter. More than you'll ever know.
1st Reporter. I don't know how we'd get along without you.

The Reporters *embrace Geraldine, then sing in close harmony*

The Music *recommences.*

1st Reporter.	Early one morning,
	Just as the sun was uppity.
2nd Reporter.	Uppity,
1st Reporter.	A maiden vanished into the blue.
Trio.	But we traced her, we chased her and fondly we embraced her
	For that maiden is our source of revenue.
	Geraldine! Geraldine!
	Geraldine, where have you been?
	We can't print a page without you;
	The boss is in a rage without you.
	Geraldine! Geraldine!
	Geraldine, the paper's queen.
	We repeat each word you utter,
	Because you are our bread and butter.
	Oh, don't deceive us
	Oh, never leave us.
	How could you use a newspaper so?
	Geraldine! Geraldine!
	Geraldine, where have you been?

Under bridges, over canyons,
We shall be your good companions,
Geraldine, Ge, Ge, Ge, Ge, Geraldine.

Geraldine! Geraldine!
Geraldine, where have you been?
Make an oath and make it solemn
That you'll be our supporting column.
Geraldine! Geraldine!

Geraldine, you're far too green,
Beauty gives you your potential,
And money makes you quite essential.
Oh, don't desert us,
Oh, never hurt us,
How could you use your news value so?

Geraldine! Geraldine!
Geraldine, you must come clean.
Tell us how you spend your Sundays,
And where you go to buy your undies.

1st Reporter. Who do you weep with?
2nd Reporter. Who do you sleep with?
3rd Reporter. Tell us who your blue sea is deep with?
Trio. Geraldine! Geraldine! Ge, Ge, Geraldine!
Ge, Ge, Ge, Ge, Geraldine! Ge, Ge, Ge, Ge, Geraldine.

GERALDINE *rises and crosses to* R. *The* REPORTERS *follow her.*

GERALDINE. Well! It's very nice of you all still to take an interest in me now that I'm penniless.
REPORTERS. Penniless?
GERALDINE. I'm very touched indeed.
2nd Reporter. What do you mean—penniless?
GERALDINE. I've given all my money away.
1st Reporter. Oh, now come, Geraldine!
2nd Reporter. Who to?
GERALDINE. I shan't say.
3rd Reporter. To charity?
2nd Reporter. To a man?
GERALDINE. No comment.
1st Reporter. I know. Jack Amersham.
GERALDINE. No comment.
3rd Reporter. If you don't tell us, we simply won't believe you.
GERALDINE. Won't you?
1st Reporter. Now, see reason, Geraldine. Tell us or we know you're just pulling a fast one.
GERALDINE. Oh, well, it was worth trying.

ALBERT *enters nervously up* L *and looks curiously around.*

Alarmed] Albert!

ALBERT, *beaming, crosses to Geraldine with outstretched hands.*

ALBERT. You remembered me! And I remembered you, too!
GERALDINE [*faintly*] Albert!
ALBERT. Yes, it's Albert. Little Cousin Geraldine! Not since we were so high, climbing trees together. And you gave me all that money.

The REPORTERS *are galvanized. They surround Albert.*

1st Reporter. It's him!

SCENE 7   FREE AS AIR

2ND REPORTER. It's you!   MUSIC
                                    Two REPORTERS *grab* ALBERT *and take him down* L. *The* 3RD
                                    REPORTER *follows.*
3RD REPORTER. What's your name, sir ?
ALBERT. Albert Postumous.
1ST REPORTER. Where do you live, Mr Postlethwaite ?
ALBERT. " Postumous."
1ST REPORTER. Are you in love with Geraldine ?
2ND REPORTER. Have you got a dear old mother ?
3RD REPORTER. Who will you marry ?
1ST REPORTER. What does it feel like to have half a million, Mr Postlethwaite ?
ALBERT. " Postumous." What ? Good heavens, no ! *Five* thousand is what—[*he crosses to Geraldine*] *dear, sweet, kind* Geraldine gave me.
1ST REPORTER. For goodness' sake !
2ND REPORTER. Geraldine, what's going on ?
GERALDINE. Are you asking me ?
2ND REPORTER. Yes.
                                    MISS CATAMOLE *enters up* L *and crosses to Geraldine.* ALBERT
                                    moves above Geraldine to L *of her.*

MISS CATAMOLE. A-ha ! You don't know me but I know you. I've got a picture of you on my mantelpiece right up in Northumberland.
GERALDINE. Northumberland ?
MISS CATAMOLE. Yes. I'm your Aunt Flo. And I've come all this way to thank you for all that money.
GERALDINE [*kissing Miss Catamole*] Dear Aunt Flo.
MISS CATAMOLE [*crossing to the Reporters*] It's a fortune. It'll make quite a bulge under the mattress.
                                    MUTCH *enters up* L *and crosses to* C.

ALBERT [*looking at Mutch*] Why, it's Uncle Jim.
GERALDINE. What ?
MUTCH [*looking around*] What ? Oh, yes. Dear Geraldine, you have provided for my old age. [*He moves down* L, *below Miss Catamole and busily shakes hands with each of the Reporters*] And are you part of the family, too ? Quite a reunion, isn't it ?
                                    POTTER *enters up* L, *carrying a bunch of flowers. He crosses
                                    straight to Geraldine and makes his speech.*

POTTER. I've brought you these flowers. Will you marry me ?
GERALDINE [*pointedly*] Cousin Howard ! Marry *me ?*
ALBERT [*sotto voce*] Wrong speech.
POTTER [*recollecting himself; carefully*] I've come all the way from Eastbourne.
GERALDINE. By air ?
POTTER. Oh, no. In Lord Paul's . . . [*He just stops himself saying " boat " and crosses down* R]
                                    LORD PAUL *enters up* L *and goes to Miss Catamole.*

LORD PAUL [*to Miss Catamole*] Ah, Geraldine, at last we meet. You are Geraldine, I suppose ? No, you're not.
GERALDINE. I'm Geraldine.
LORD PAUL [*crossing to Geraldine*] Splendid ! [*He kisses her*] Never set eyes on you before, of course, but you remembered your father's old friend. Charming gesture.
GERALDINE. Oh, it *was* nothing.
LORD PAUL. Can't accept it, of course.
GERALDINE. Oh, he would have wished it.
LORD PAUL. Well, in that case . . . [*He crosses to Potter*]
                                    JACK *and* MOLLY *enter up* L. *She carries a small box and a pile
                                    of letters.* JACK *wears a false moustache and carries a stick.*
                                    MOLLY *stands in the doorway.* JACK *limps with his stick to
                                    Geraldine.*

56　　　　　　　　　　　　　FREE AS AIR　　　　　　　　　　　　　ACT II

GERALDINE. Dear old Uncle Jack. You shouldn't have come all this way.　　　MUSIC
JACK. Why not?
GERALDINE. With your poor slipped disc.

JACK walks very lamely.

JACK. Is it?
GERALDINE. And your rheumatism.

JACK grows even more lame.

And for a mere fifty thousand.

JACK sits on a stool at the bar.

MOLLY [*crossing to Geraldine*] Cousin Geraldine, we got together to try to show you our gratitude. [*She gives Geraldine the box*] This is a little present with love, gratitude and best wishes from all of your family favourites—[*She gives Geraldine the letters*] and these are some letters from those of the family who could not be present.
JACK. It isn't rheumatism, it's writer's cramp.

GERALDINE opens the box. It contains the turtle pendant.

1ST REPORTER. Look here, Geraldine, I thought you had no family.

The REPORTERS barge their way c and surround Geraldine.

GERALDINE. I didn't know I had. A legacy brings them all out, doesn't it?
2ND REPORTER. You know this'll kill you, don't you? You'll die in a tiny paragraph on the back page.
GERALDINE. Sounds a peaceful death.
JACK. Are these friends of yours, Geraldine?
1ST REPORTER. No, we're not friends. I am on the staff of the *Daily Echo*.
ALBERT. The *Daily Echo!* Oh, we're *so* grateful. We should never have found Geraldine but for you.
JACK. You told us where she was and what she did.
ALBERT. Three cheers for the *Daily Echo*. Hip, hip . . .

ALL except the REPORTERS give three cheers.

JACK. Let's pretend they're relations and buy them all a drink.
MISS CATAMOLE. That's it. Come along now. The drink's free. Everything's free.

REPRISE
No. 23
"FREE TO SING"
ENSEMBLE

MUTCH.	North!
ALL.	*Bong!*
MUTCH.	South!
ALL.	*Bong!*
MUTCH.	East!
ALL.	*Bong!*
MUTCH.	West!
ALL.	*Bong!*
	Free to sing, free to go
	North and South and ev'rywhere.

The REPORTERS exit.

Free as air that will cost you nothing
Free as air bom-pa—bom—bom—bom.
GERALDINE [*speaking over the music*] Oh, what a wonderful idea. Who thought of it?

ALL. I did!
ALBERT. Will you come home now?
GERALDINE. Oh, yes. Thank you. [*She sings*]
GERALDINE. Follow me, follow me,
Merrily because,
ALL. *Bong!*
Thought is free,
Speech is free,
Ev'rything is free.

ALL *dance off up* L *as—*

the FRONT CLOTH *falls*

The MUSIC *continues.*

SCENE 8

The Shore Front Cloth. A little later that evening.

ALBERT *and* GERALDINE *enter* L, *dance across and exit* R. *They are followed by* LORD PAUL, MUTCH *and* MOLLY *chased by* JACK. *They all exit* R. MISS CATAMOLE *and* POTTER *enter hand-in-hand* L *and cross to* C.

The MUSIC *fades.*

POTTER. Home.
MISS CATAMOLE. Thank goodness.
POTTER. It was dreadful.
MISS CATAMOLE. And so dangerous.
POTTER. The noise! [*He puts his fingers in his ears*]
MISS CATAMOLE. And all those posters telling you what to do.
POTTER. Would you mind repeating that? I think I've gone deaf.
MISS CATAMOLE. No, dear, you haven't. [*She takes Potter's hands from his ears*]

"WE'RE HOLDING HANDS" No. 24

MISS CATAMOLE *and* POTTER

BOTH. I always knew that you cared for me,
We've shared a happy past,
But I thought it was just for the twenty-odd years
I didn't believe it would last.
I didn't know it was more than that,
I never understood,
For I knew that I had you for better or worse,
But not that I had you for good.

We're holding hands!
Things are getting serious.
We're holding hands!
Life is most mysterious!
You've never done that before.
MISS CATAMOLE. You've only raised your hat before.
POTTER. But now I'll be lingering at your door.
BOTH. Now that we're holding hands.
Holding, holding hands,
Now that we're holding hands.

		MUSIC
	We're holding hands!	
	Things are moving fast for us.	
	We're holding hands!	
	Love has come at last for us.	
	You've never done this before.	
Miss Catamole.	You've never been remiss before.	
	But now you'll be wanting a kiss—or more,	
Both.	Now that we're holding hands,	
	Holding, holding hands,	
	Now that we're holding hands.	

Miss Catamole *and* Potter *exit* R.

Scene 9

The Well. Sunset.

The well is more elaborately decorated and a string of bunting is slung between the houses R *and* L. *There is a bench* R *and the barrel is* L. *The stocks are in front of the well.*

When the Front Cloth *rises,* Ivy *is walking about, crying softly. She glances off* L, *sees someone coming, hurriedly sits and puts her feet back into the stocks. This she does quite easily by taking off her shoes.* Lord Paul *enters up* L *and crosses to Ivy.*

Lord Paul. Miss Crush! Miss Crush! You're crying.
Ivy. I know.
Lord Paul [*unlocking the stocks*] And no wonder. These barbarous customs. It was dreadful to treat you so. [*He helps Ivy to rise*]
Ivy. No, I *liked* the stocks. That isn't why I'm crying. It's all the harm I've done here.
Lord Paul. Harm?
Ivy. Miss Melford having to go and everyone so upset and then it started to rain.
Lord Paul. But Miss Melford's come back and everyone's *un*upset.
Ivy. Really?
Lord Paul. And it's stopped raining. And you were only doing this remarkable job of yours.
Ivy. That's what I thought, but now I feel ashamed. I've got fond of the island—and people. People don't realize how quickly I get fond of people.
Lord Paul. Then stay, Miss Crush. Stay and be my wife. What am I saying? Yes, be my wife. You bolster up my ego. I haven't riches, I'm afraid. There *is* a little family silver—but of course you saw it at breakfast.

Ivy *bursts into tears.*

Why are you crying?
Ivy. Because you've forgiven me.
Lord Paul. And will you marry me?
Ivy [*blowing her nose*] Oh, yes. Thank you very much.
Lord Paul. Splendid! And you can protect me from women, as you said.
Ivy. Oh, I'll protect you from everything, Lord Paul. Oh! Shall I be Lady Ivy?
Lord Paul. No. Ivy, Lady Postumous.
Ivy. Fancy! Life's just beginning and it sounds as if I were dead.

"TERHOU"   No. 25

Molly and The Company

Lord Paul [*speaking over the music*] Heavens! The Coronation. Come on, we shall be late.

Lord Paul *and* Ivy *exit hurriedly down* L.

SCENE 9 — FREE AS AIR

Four ISLAND GIRLS *enter. Two of them carry lighted lanterns which they hang on wall hooks* R *and* L, *then exit. The other two collect the stocks and exit with them, leaving the cushions on the well.*

MOLLY *enters up* L *and crosses to* R.

MOLLY [*singing*]
Terhou! Terhou!
The winter sea is grey
And wild your winter day
For ever.
In April blue
The clouds that wander free
Are shadows on the sea,
For ever.

The Coronation procession enters up L, *led by* LORD PAUL *who carries a crown of flowers.* ALBERT, MUTCH, POTTER *and* MISS CATAMOLE *come next, then* GERALDINE, *with two* ISLAND GIRLS *in attendance.* BINDWEED, TOM *and* GREGORY *follow with the remaining* ISLAND GIRLS *and* MEN *behind.* IVY *and* JACK *come last. The ceremony has simplicity and dignity but is not solemn. The procession circles the stage then* LORD PAUL *gives his hand to* GERALDINE, *seats her on the well and places the crown of flowers on her head. This business is completed as the singing finishes.*

Summer hails
The swallow flying home.
White as breaking foam
The seabird sails.
Terhou! Terhou! In silence and alone
The ocean is your own, For ever.

Terhou! Terhou!
The winter sea is grey,
And wild your winter day
For ever.
In April blue
The clouds that wander free
Are shadows on the sea, For ever.

Summer hails
The swallow flying home.
White as breaking foam
The seabird sails.

Terhou! Terhou! In silence and alone
The ocean is your own, For ever.
MOLLY. For ever.

The MUSIC *continues.*

MISS CATAMOLE [*speaking over the music*] Well, that's over.
LORD PAUL. For another year. [*Lightly*] God save the Queen!

MISS CATAMOLE *kisses* GERALDINE.

GREGORY [*moving to Molly*] Molly!

MOLLY *moves up* R *to Jack. There is general movement. Two or three* ISLAND GIRLS *exit* R *and re-enter with trays of mugs. An* ISLAND MAN *exits* L *and re-enters with a tray of mugs.*

LORD PAUL. Now, before we—er—start the party, I want you all to know that Miss Crush has consented to be my wife.

ALL [*ad lib*] Well, I never did. Congratulations. [*Etc., etc.*]
POTTER [R] That reminds me of something.
MISS CATAMOLE [*crossing to Potter*] Yes, Mr Potter, you did ask me. Do you remember what I replied?
POTTER. Perfectly.
ALBERT [*shaking hands with Lord Paul*] Thank you very much. I mean—congratulations. I mean—that sets me free. [*He turns to Geraldine*] Geraldine, I love you.
GERALDINE. And I love you, Albert.
ALBERT. Will you marry me?
GERALDINE. If you won't think it's just for your money.

There is general laughter. The drinks are distributed.

MISS CATAMOLE. Whatever will you do with all that money?
ALBERT [*practically*] I thought I'd buy a horse to bring things up from the beach.
MISS CATAMOLE. Oh, what a good idea.
MUTCH [LC] A mule would be better.
ALBERT. You think so?
POTTER [*crossing to Mutch*] Oh, no, a horse.
MUTCH. A mule. There's been a mule here before.
LORD PAUL [*joining Mutch and Potter*] When? Not in my time.
MUTCH. Of course not. But my grandfather talked of a mule.
A GIRL. Horses are prettier.

Everyone talks at once. The MEN *go into a huddle* L *and the* GIRLS *group* R. MOLLY *moves down* C, *weeping.*

JACK [*following Molly*] What's the matter, Molly? What is it? [*Loudly*] Will someone tell me why Molly's crying? An hour ago she consented to come away with me.

The MUSIC *ceases.*

MOLLY [*crying*] I don't want to go, now.
JACK. Oh, Molly, *come*. You said of all things you wanted to go to the mainland.
MOLLY [*still crying*] But I hadn't been then. I don't like it.
JACK. You wanted bright lights.
MOLLY. I didn't know they'd be as bright as that.
JACK. And you wanted *me*.
MOLLY. Over there you're just like everyone else.

GREGORY *moves tentatively forward to comfort* MOLLY, *who joins him* RC *and takes his hand.*

JACK. For Heaven's sake, what *do* you want, then?

FINALE   No. 26

THE COMPANY

MOLLY [*over the music*] All I know is [*she sings*]
    I don't want a man from the mainland,
    It was madness, it was folly.
    And I'll never think of Jack again.
    It was wrong, wrong, wrong.

ALL.   She's tired of the man from the mainland,
    So we won't be losing Molly,
    For she's well and truly back again,
    Where she should belong.

The MUSIC *continues.*

SCENE 9   FREE AS AIR

GERALDINE [*over the music*] Never mind, Jack.
JACK. Good-bye, Molly. [*He kisses her*] It was the sweetest romance of all, and the shortest. Good-bye, Geraldine. I hope I shall be able to forgive you for everything. [*He kisses Geraldine*]
GERALDINE. We'll see you to the boat.
JACK. Oh, no, you won't. It would spoil the party. You can wave to me.
LORD PAUL [*through the megaphone*] Tom!
TOM [*moving to R of Lord Paul*] Aye, aye, Lord Paul.
LORD PAUL. Ready?
TOM. Aye, aye.

> TOM *and* JACK *go up* R *on to the rostrum, cross at the back and exit over the wall up* L. *The others move up and wave to him over the wall.*

ISLAND MAN [*singing*]
    The boat's in!
    What's the boat brought in?

> *The* COMPANY *move down and group.*

ALL.   A sack of flour
    And a lady.
    The boat's in
    With the paraffin
    And a rolling pin
    And a lady
SOLOIST.   A bottle of ink
    And a kitchen sink
ALL.   A case of wine
    And a ball of twine
    A cutter for the ditches
    And a pair of leather breeches
    And a lady,
    And a lady, lady, lady, lady, lady.

    The boat's in.
    What's the boat brought in?
    A frying-pan
    And a lady.
    The boat's in
    With a baking tin
    And a tarpaulin
    And a lady.
SOLOIST.   A razor blade
    And a garden spade,
ALL.   A coil of rope
    And a box of soap,
    A bottle with a stopper
    And a hammer and a chopper.

> ALL *raise their mugs to Geraldine.*

    And a lady,
    And a lady, lady, lady, lady, lady.

CURTAIN

MUSIC FOR CURTAIN CALLS

REPRISE

" I'M UP EARLY "

The Company

ALL.
We're up early
To greet the day
To smell the air, to feel the breeze,
To hear the rustling in the trees,
This morning.
We're up early
We couldn't sleep
We woke up dreaming something sweet;
We'll smile at ev'ryone we meet
This morning.

Ev'rywhere
A stir is in the air.
Ev'rything
Is telling us it's Spring.

We're up early
To see the sun.
We know that he is here to stay,
We know what we mean by May
This morning,
Because it's that kind of a morning
It's that kind of a morning
It's that kind of a morning
This morning.

REPRISE

" A MAN FROM THE MAINLAND "

The Company

GIRLS.
We want a man from the mainland,
He has rent us half asunder
And our souls will all be saleable
For a mainland kiss.

We all want a man from the mainland,
We will swamp him till he's under
And we'll nail him if he's nailable
To an island miss.

MEN.
Take them away
Take them to London.
They're tied up in knots
And ready to be undone.

GIRLS.
Hurry! Hurry! Oh!

		MUSIC
GIRLS.	We ⎫ all want a man from the mainland	
MEN.	They ⎭	

And we must say we don't wonder
When we think of what's available
In a place like this.

REPRISE   No. 29

"LET THE GRASS GROW"

THE COMPANY

ALL.   Let the grass grow under your feet
Till it grows knee deep,
Let the bright day amble along
Till it ends in sleep.
A man's life is very quickly over
Make time last by wandering through the clover.
Let the grass grow under your feet
Give it a chance to grow until it grows knee deep.

LORD PAUL.   Deeper, deeper, deeper, deeper, deeper, deeper, deeper,
ALL.   Give it a chance to grow until it grows knee deep.
LORD PAUL.   Give it a chance to grow,
ALL.   Knee deep.

FINAL CURTAIN

PLAY-OUT MUSIC

REPRISE   No. 30

"I'M UP EARLY"

FURNITURE AND PROPERTY LIST

ACT I

Scene 1

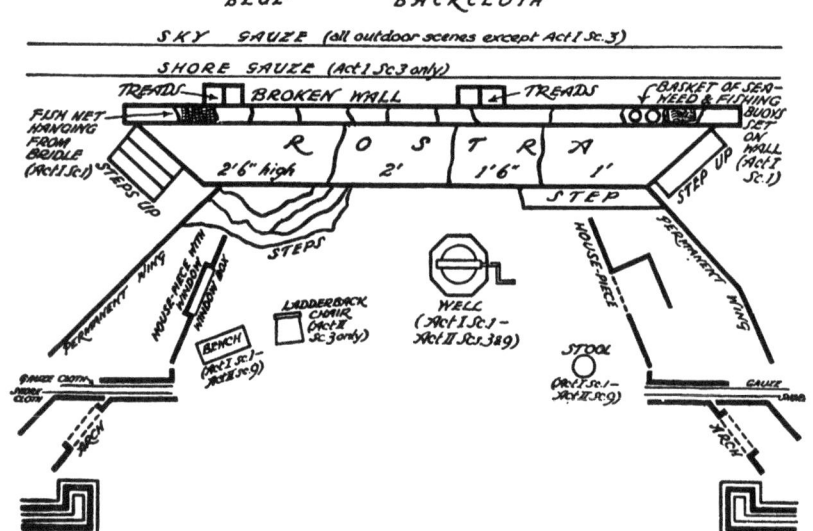

On stage—Bench (R). *On it:* milk-jug with beaded cover, 3 tea-towels
    Stool (L). *On it:* small metal milk-churn
    On bridle up R: fishing-net
    On wall up L: 3 fish-boxes, basket of seaweed
    Well with bucket

Off stage—Small milk-churn and ladle (MUTCH)
    Small bowl, towel (POTTER)
    Spade, duster (GREGORY)

Fish-baskets, brooms, bowls, scrubbing-brushes, washing-baskets (ISLANDERS)
Knitting-bag with knitting (MISS CATAMOLE)
2 cups of tea (MISS CATAMOLE)
Petticoat (ISLAND GIRL)
Walking-stick, telescope, recorder, megaphone (LORD PAUL)

Personal—MUTCH: pipe, tobacco, matches

Scene 2

Front Cloth   No Properties

FREE AS AIR

Scene 3

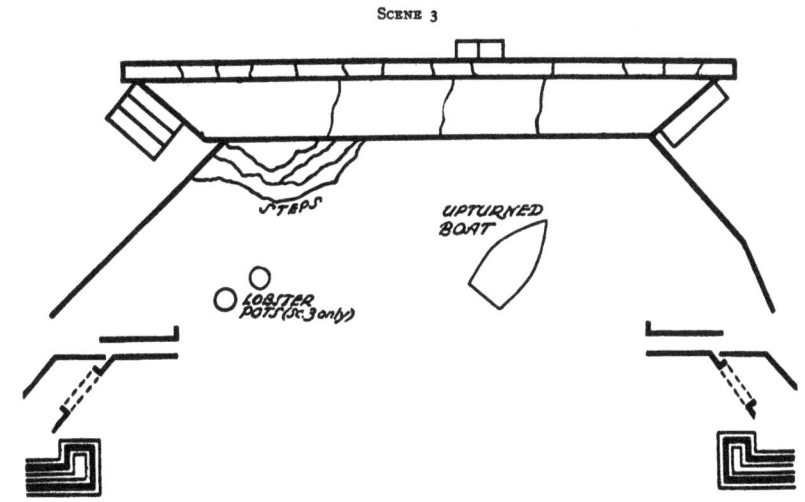

On stage—Upturned boat
    3 lobster pots
    3 suitcases
    Boat's mast
    Fishing-nets
Behind wall: paraffin can, rolling-pin, bottle of ink, case of wine, ball of twine, ditch-cutter, leather breeches, frying pan, baking tin, razor blade, bottle with stopper

Off stage—Knitting (Miss Catamole)
    List of names (Albert)

Personal—Geraldine: handbag
    Mutch: pencil and paper

Scene 4

Off stage—Wheelbarrow (Bindweed)
    2 stools (Gregory)
    Garland (Gregory)
    Flowers (Molly)

SCENE 5

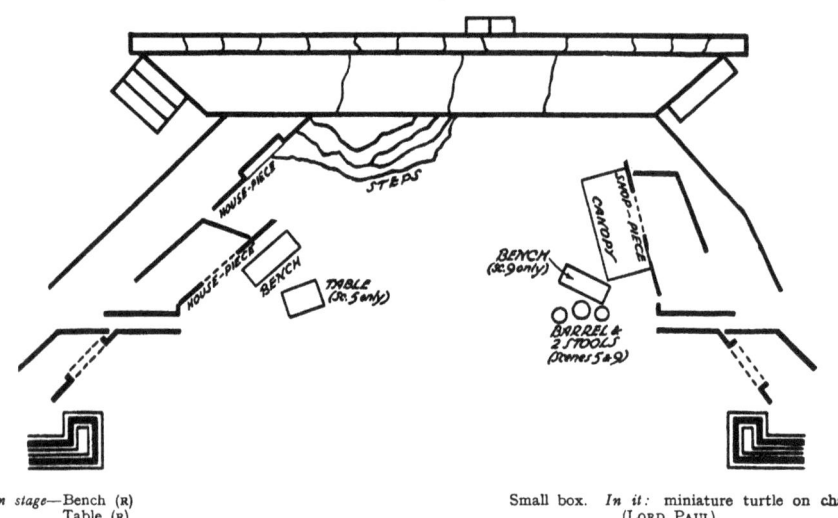

On stage—Bench (R)
　　　　　Table (R)
　　　　　Barrel (L)
　　　　　2 stools (L)
　　　　　Inside shop L: bottle of beer, 2 glasses

Off stage—Megaphone (LORD PAUL)
　　　　　Document, bottle of ink, pen (POTTER)

Small box. In it: miniature turtle on chain
　　　　　　　　　　　　　　(LORD PAUL)
Drum and beater (MUTCH)
Cider flagon, 2 cups (GIRL)
Hat, mirror (GERALDINE)
Stole (MISS CATAMOLE)
Knitting (MISS CATAMOLE)

Personal—LORD PAUL: recorder, handkerchief

SCENE 6

Personal—LORD PAUL: handkerchief, watch

SCENE 7

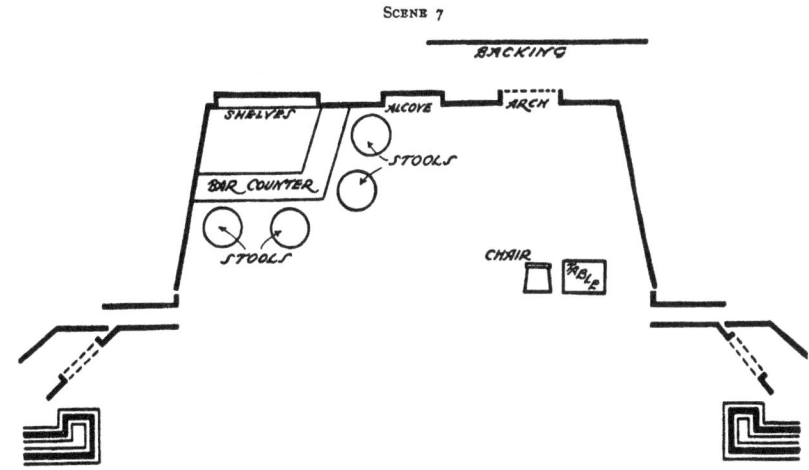

On stage—Bar. *On it:* glasses, ashtrays, mats, telephone, bell
Shelves. *On them:* bottles, glasses
4 high stools
Table
Chair

Behind bar: tray with 9 whiskies
bottle of port
bottle of whisky
clean glass

Off stage—2 suitcases (IVY)
Goggles, garland (JACK)
Boat-hook (LORD PAUL)

SCENE 8

Off stage—2 suitcases (LORD PAUL)
Pitchfork (BINDWEED)

Oar (TOM)
Lantern (MUTCH)

SCENE 9

On stage—Bench (R)
Bench (L)

Barrell (L). *On it:* lantern, tray with 4 glasses of cider
2 stools

ACT II

SCENE 1

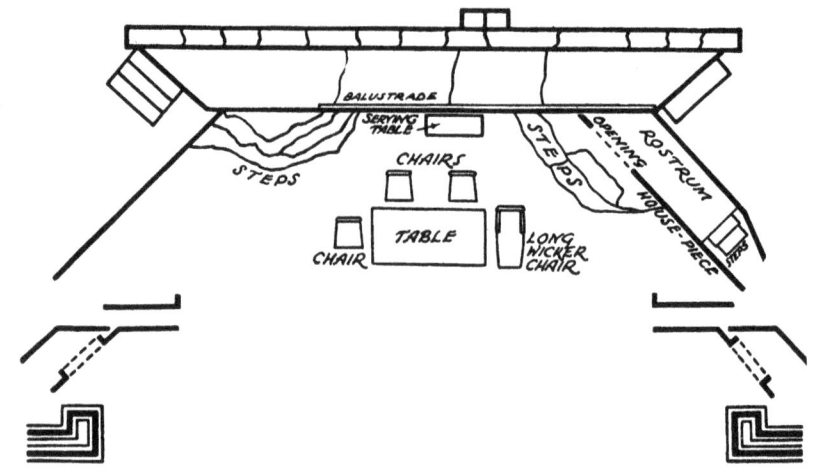

On stage—Table. *On it:* white lace cloth, 4 knives, 4 small plates, 3 cups, 3 saucers, 3 teaspoons, dish of marmalade, rack with toast, plate with 8 oranges, copy of " The Geographical Magazine "
Serving-table. *On it:* hot-plate with a pot of coffee and a silver dish and cover; jug of milk, sugar basin, cup, saucer, teaspoon
Under it: tray
Long wicker chair. *On it:* Lord Paul's jacket
3 upright chairs
Speaking tube

Off stage—Notebook and pencil (IVY)
Dish of butter (ALBERT)

Personal—IVY : sun-glasses
ALBERT : butler's apron

SCENE 2

Front Cloth   No Properties

SCENE 3

On stage—Ladder-back chair (R). *On it:* knitting
Well. *On it:* seaweed
Basket (L). *In it:* seaweed

Off stage—Books (LORD PAUL)
Tape-recorder (IVY)
Notebook and pencil (IVY)

Camera (IVY)
Long piece of seaweed (POTTER)
Megaphone (LORD PAUL)
Pitch pipe (MUTCH)
Stocks (POTTER)
Cushions (TOM)
Crumpled piece of paper (TOM)

SCENE 4

Personal—GERALDINE : letter

FREE AS AIR

SCENE 5

On stage—Upturned boat
          Lobster pots (R)

Off stage—3 suitcases (TOM)
          Boat's mast
          Fishing-nets

SCENE 6

Personal—ALBERT: cheque and letter

SCENE 7

Same setting as Act I Scene 7
On shelves: bottle of whisky, 3 glasses
Off stage—Bunch of flowers (POTTER)
          Box. *In it:* turtle pendant (MOLLY)

          Letters (MOLLY)

Personal—1ST REPORTER: telegram
          JACK: false moustache, stick

SCENE 8

No properties

SCENE 9

On stage—Well (decorated)
          Bunting
          Stocks
          Cushions
          Bench (R)
          Barrel (L)

Off stage—2 lanterns (ISLAND GIRLS)
          Crown of flowers (LORD PAUL)
          3 trays with 11 mugs (ISLAND GIRLS)
          1 tray with 10 mugs (ISLAND MAN)

LIGHTING PLOT

ACT I SCENE 1 Exterior Morning
Property Fittings Required—none
The Main Acting Areas Cover—the whole stage
To open: Effect of early morning sunrise
No cues

ACT I SCENE 2 Front Cloth
To open: Effect of morning sunshine
No cues

ACT I SCENE 3 The Seashore
Property Fittings Required—none
The Main Acting Areas Are—RC, LC, C and up C.
To open: Effect of morning sunshine
No cues

ACT I SCENE 4 Front Cloth
To open: Effect of bright sunshine
No cues

ACT I SCENE 5 Exterior
Property Fittings Required—none
The Main Acting Areas Are—the whole stage
To open: Effect of late afternoon sunshine
No cues

ACT I SCENE 6 Front Cloth
To open: Effect of early evening twilight
Cue 1   At end of Scene   (page 25)
           BLACK-OUT

ACT I SCENE 7 Interior A Bar Evening
Property Fittings Required—none
The Main Acting Areas Are—C, up R and down L
To open: Effect of artificial light
Cue 2   At end of Scene   (page 31)
           BLACK-OUT

ACT I SCENE 8 Front Cloth Night
To open: Effect of moonlight
Cue 3   At end of Scene   (page 32)
           BLACK-OUT

ACT I SCENE 9 Exterior Night
The Apparent Sources of Light Are—moonlight and a lantern L
To open: Effect of moonlight
Cue 4   During Scene
           Periodic lighthouse flashes

ACT II SCENE 1 Exterior Morning
To open: Effect of morning sunshine
No cues

ACT II SCENE 2 Front Cloth
To open: Effect of morning sunshine
Cue 5   At end of Scene   (page 40)
           BLACK-OUT

ACT II SCENE 3
Same setting as Act I Scene 1
To open: Effect of morning sunshine
No cues

ACT II SCENE 4 Front Cloth
To open: Effect of misty daylight
No cues

ACT II SCENE 5 The Seashore Afternoon
To open: Effect of misty daylight
No cues

ACT II SCENE 6 Front Cloth
To open: Effect of misty daylight
Cue 6   At end of Scene   (page 52)
           Dim lights to BLACK-OUT

ACT II SCENE 7 The Bar
To open: Effect of artificial light
No cues

ACT II SCENE 8 Front Cloth
To open: Effect of just before sunset
No cues

ACT II SCENE 9
Same setting as Act I Scene 1
To open: effect of sunset
No cues

MADE AND PRINTED IN GREAT BRITAIN BY
LATIMER TREND & COMPANY LTD PLYMOUTH
MADE IN ENGLAND

www.ingramcontent.com/pod-product-compliance
Ingram Content Group UK Ltd.
Pitfield, Milton Keynes, MK11 3LW, UK
UKHW021846210426
5322IPUK00022B/489